Living Into the Narrative of God

Reverend Cari Willis

Dear Mark,
Here's to the new life
you are building that I
pray will be full of love,
affection, fun + Enjoy the
journey, + may your continue too.
spiritual growth written by my
this book is my dew
friend is my dew
favorite —
you are loved +
Jappreciated !
Mary M.
6/21

Contents

Thank you

I am very grateful to my many friends who have made this book happen for me. I am very fortunate to have many friends behind the walls of the prison who have shaped me as a person and as a minister. I am lucky to have them to dialog with, to write to, to listen to, to discuss deep theological thoughts with, and wellllllll, just to laugh with. I also deeply appreciate all of my students who have taken my "Living into the Narrative of God" class. I learned more from them, I am sure, than they learned from me.

I am deeply indebted to Reverend Lynn McLaughlin who I worked with on our first class with the prison. Having her as my co-teacher was more than I could ask for. She reminds me every time I see her what it looks like and what it means to be Christ for another person.

I am very grateful to Mike Boyd for sharing with me the cover art, a scene in the Indiana Dunes State Park near Chesterton, Indiana. I told him the picture that I had in my mind and just a few minutes later he sent the exact photograph I wanted! God does indeed work in miraculous ways! Mike also lent me his extensive knowledge as an editor to make this book sing!

This book was profoundly shaped by these relationships and friendships; I am forever grateful to God for these amazing people: Wolfgang, Ken, Mike, Cathy, Barb, Ricky, Joan, Douglas, Susan, Ronnie, Kathy, Mark, Lisa, Jingsong, Thomas, my friends at the women's prison, and all of my friends at the Federal prison.

PART 1. INTRODUCTION

Overview

Live into the narrative of God: What does it mean?

What does it mean to "live into the narrative of God"? It means immersing yourself into the Scriptural text in order to receive a word from God just for you. It means putting the text on as you would your own clothing to see how it looks. It means walking around in the scene. It means play acting each character to such a depth that the character's persona becomes your persona. After all these things, then you try to feel, sense, smell, see, touch, and hear all that is going on in the scene before you, so that God can speak directly to you.

Living into the narrative of God also means listening to the sacred story as if you were hearing it for the very first time. It means bringing to the text a posture of hearing it as a child would at the feet of a beloved grandparent. In so doing, there is an awe and an excited expectation for what comes next – what new twist in the story will happen, which character will I fall in love with, and how will the story end.

Living into the narrative of God means that you will allow Scripture to interpret your life. If you are familiar with the ancient Jewish practice of Midrash, you know how Scripture can interpret other Scriptures. In this practice, you will learn how various Scriptures can interpret you by asking questions of the text in order to illuminate your life, your relationship with God, and your theological views!

Living into the narrative of God means that you have to be vulnerable and open to all feelings and thoughts that come up – good or bad, happy or sad, wanted or unwanted – as gifts from God. You have to be ready to ask the surprising questions of the text that you might not have thought you were ready for in order to find the deeper truths about yourself and your relationship with God.

Lectio Divina

This practice is not new! Some folks call this *Lectio Divina*. I have found, though, that those two words can be off-putting to some people and the participants won't even listen to the next word or two about the spiritual practice. However, telling someone to simply *be* with the text sounds a lot less threatening and a whole lot less difficult.

Most *Lectio* practices will have you do the hard work of coming up with "the word" in the Scriptural text that you feel your heart is most in tune with as well as to ask you to ask your own questions of the text. This often seems way too daunting to people who are beginning the practice. They give up before they even start! In this book, I attempt to help you, the reader, start the practice so that you can see how transformational it can be for your life.

For my own life, there is no other spiritual practice, other than centering prayer, that is more transformational for my relationship with God. Seeing myself in the Scriptural narrative of God – truly being in the scene with Jesus – helped me to see Jesus' love and mercy in a whole new light. I pray this book will help you gain your footing within the narrative of God so your life will be transformed as well.

How to get started

Here is the way to get started.

- First, take a deep breath. Then read the Scriptural text once through. Try to read it as if you have never heard the story before. In this way, you lean in and try to pick up on the story's nuances.
- Close your eyes and imagine yourself there. Try to just *be* in the scene without thinking too much about it.
- After a few minutes of just *being* with the Scriptural text, read the Scriptural text again. This time, read it at a much slower pace. Pay attention to even the small words like "but," "now," "yet," or "all."
- After reading the text, close your eyes again. Imagine yourself as one of the characters, and play-act the entire scene through. Then, switch to another character, and play-act the entire scene through again. Do this until you have played all of the characters.

  If the Scriptural text has a "crowd" in the scene, you can envision yourself as a person close to the action and then another person far away straining to see what is going on.

- Now, settle in on one character in the Scripture that grabs you the most.

  Think to yourself: "Why does this character have my attention?"

  "What is surprising me?"

  "What makes me ask: 'What did they just say? What does *that* mean?'"

- At this point, you might want to say a short prayer such as: "Gracious God, open my eyes, so that I can see the truth of you, the truth of me, and the truth of you and me."
- Read the Scripture text one more time. Again, read it at a slow pace.

  I have provided phrase-by-phrase readings of each Scriptural text in order to help you slow down, stop, and think about what each element says. If something makes your heart leap or stop as you read the Scripture, write that thought or feeling down in the empty space.

  Be intentional about being *slow* as you read the story. Read it. Reflect on what you read. Read the next bit of text. Then reflect on it. Write down any impressions as you go. Remember: All emotions, positive or negative, are wanted; welcome your emotions with grace as you write them down.

- I have provided for you a list of questions. Read each question one by one. Answer each question that especially makes your heart skip a beat or makes your breath come up short. Not all questions prompt **Aha**! But a few will.

  And a few will lead you to deeper questions that you will have.

  Write those deeper questions down.

  Write your thoughts down.

  Do not edit yourself. It's important to allow yourself to just *be* with the text and see what God has to show you.

- To fully live into the narrative, take those initial thoughts and feelings to write a short story. Express all that you have seen, heard, and felt. Share how, as you listened in on the scene, that you received a word from God. Talk about how your life was transformed by the whole experience.

- Now, go back and think about how you can take on "the mind of Christ" by thinking about being Jesus in the scene. Journal for yourself the ways in which you have and have not been Jesus. If you need to, repent to God for the ways that you feel you have fallen short. Then, put together a simple list of a few ways you will commit to in order to be more like Christ each day.

I have included short stories of my own based on my living into the narrative of God. My stories might give a sense of how you can take even the littlest of phrases and create a whole story around it. I hope that the stories also help you see how you can take one question that God or Jesus asks and feel it as a personal question asked just to you.

You will be given space to write your own story within this book. Obviously, you can decide whether you want to write your story within this book or whether you would rather keep a writing journal that will contain your stories.

A note for pastors

- I suggest that you read the text slowly and think not only of yourself in the narrative, but consider your congregation members.
    - How would Ps. 23:2 "He maketh me lie down" sound to your parishioner who was just told he has to have yet another surgery? To the new mother-to-be who was told that she is on complete bed rest? To the star athlete who just injured his leg?
    - Jesus asks, "Do you see this woman (man)?" (Luke 7:44) How does that sound to the woman who comes in late, sits on the back row, and leaves early before anyone can greet her? How does it sound to the woman who is struggling with depression? How does it sound to the man struggling with drug and alcohol addictions?
- In other words: Walk around in other people's skin, in other people's life stories, and in other people's life consequences. Hear how the story will affect them. Hear how it might be very good news or the worst news possible.
- Understand how your congregation members might have been marginalized and read the text with that lens:
    - Have they been judged because of their multiple incarcerations?
    - Will no one accept them because of their sexual orientation?
    - Is there a history of abuse that has brought about years of shame and self-rejection?
    - Do they have mental health issues that no one wants to understand?

I have included sermons that I have preached to those in prison or as I term it "those on the inside." I include these in order to show how the sermon can take on a different life because the Scriptural text has been lived into, based upon a marginalized congregation.

PART 2. SCRIPTURE, QUESTIONS, AND STORIES

Luke 15:1-10

We start with the familiar story of the lost sheep and the lost coin. Remember, for your first step, you are just going to get comfortable where you are, read the Scripture, and imagine yourself within it. Then, allow yourself just to *be* with it for 5-10 minutes. You might want to notice words or phrases that catch your eye. As best as you can, hear this story as if you never heard it before – as if it is completely new.

[1] Now the tax collectors and sinners were all gathering around to hear Jesus. [2] But the Pharisees and the teachers of the law muttered, "This man welcomes sinners and eats with them." [3] Then Jesus told them this parable: [4] "Suppose one of you has a hundred sheep and loses one of them. Doesn't he leave the ninety-nine in the open country and go after the lost sheep until he finds it? [5] And when he finds it, he joyfully puts it on his shoulders [6] and goes home. Then he calls his friends and neighbors together and says, 'Rejoice with me; I have found my lost sheep.' [7] I tell you that in the same way there will be more rejoicing in heaven over one sinner who repents than over ninety-nine righteous persons who do not need to repent. [8] "Or suppose a woman has ten silver coins and loses one. Doesn't she light a lamp, sweep the house and search carefully until she finds it? [9] And when she finds it, she calls her friends and neighbors together and says, 'Rejoice with me; I have found my lost coin.' [10] In the same way, I tell you, there is rejoicing in the presence of the angels of God over one sinner who repents."

Phrase by phrase

Now, slow down and read the story phrase by phrase. Write down anything that pops into your head, especially anything that surprises you as you read each phrase. There might be wanted and unwanted feelings that pop up; write those feelings down and welcome them into this time and space. You might want to say a short prayer; "Thank you, Lord, for all that you will reveal about myself and about you through this Scripture." Usually, I read the Scripture this way two times so I can really let it soak in.

[1] Now the tax collectors and sinners

were all gathering around to hear Jesus.

[2] But the Pharisees and the teachers

of the law muttered,

"This man welcomes sinners

and eats with them."

[3] Then Jesus told them this parable:

[4] "Suppose one of you has a hundred sheep

and loses one of them.

Doesn't he leave the ninety-nine

in the open country

and go after the lost sheep

until he finds it?

[5] And when he finds it,

he joyfully puts it on his shoulders

[6] and goes home.

Then he calls his friends

and neighbors together

and says, 'Rejoice with me;

I have found my lost sheep.'

[7] I tell you that in the same way

there will be more rejoicing in heaven

over one sinner who repents

than over ninety-nine righteous persons

who do not need to repent.

[8] "Or suppose a woman

has ten silver coins

and loses one.

Doesn't she light a lamp,

sweep the house

and search carefully

until she finds it?

[9] And when she finds it,

she calls her friends

and neighbors together

and says, 'Rejoice with me;

I have found my lost coin.'

[10] In the same way, I tell you,

there is rejoicing

in the presence of the angels of God

over one sinner who repents."

Questions of the text

Now, read the Scripture slowly again, and then ask questions of the Scripture. Only one or two of the questions offered below will jump out at you. Concentrate on just those few questions; ask yourself why it is that they beg for your attention. These questions might bring up other questions in your mind; write those down in the space provided. The questions again might bring up wanted and unwanted feelings; I encourage you to welcome both types of feelings with grace.

> [1] Now the tax collectors and sinners were all gathering around to hear Jesus. [2] But the Pharisees and the teachers of the law muttered, "This man welcomes sinners and eats with them." [3] Then Jesus told them this parable: [4] "Suppose one of you has a hundred sheep and loses one of them. Doesn't he leave the ninety-nine in the open country and go after the lost sheep until he finds it? [5] And when he finds it, he joyfully puts it on his shoulders [6] and goes home. Then he calls his friends and neighbors together and says, 'Rejoice with me; I have found my lost sheep.' [7] I tell you that in the same way there will be more rejoicing in heaven over one sinner who repents than over ninety-nine righteous persons who do not need to repent. [8] "Or suppose a woman has ten silver coins and loses one. Doesn't she light a lamp, sweep the house and search carefully until she finds it? [9] And when she finds it, she calls her friends and neighbors together and says, 'Rejoice with me; I have found my lost coin.' [10] In the same way, I tell you, there is rejoicing in the presence of the angels of God over one sinner who repents."

1. Put yourself in the narrative. Where are you in the scene?
   - Are you sitting with the Pharisees or are you sitting with the sinners?
   - Are you hanging out along the fringes of the crowd of sinners looking for a bit of grace and mercy?
   - What does it feel like to be the Pharisee?

- What does it feel like to be the sinner?
- Do you stay away from those on the fringe of society? If so, what keeps you away?
- Who are the "neighbors" that you would call to your celebration?

2. Imagine yourself as the sheep who has lost its way.
   - What do your new surroundings look like? Is it storming? Is it dangerous? Are there rock formations that you have to traverse over? Is it flat land? Is there water nearby?
   - What does it feel like to be lost?
   - What does it feel like to be separated from the flock of other sheep?
     - Do you feel free?
     - Do you feel so very, very lost?
     - Do you feel abandoned by the other sheep? Do you feel abandoned by the shepherd?
   - How long have you been lost?
   - Did you run away? If so, what has caused you to run away from the other 99 sheep?
     - Is there something about the community of 99 that compels you to run?
     - Have you ever experienced a time when you were a part of a community and you could no longer stand to be with them? What was that like?
     - Have you ever run away intentionally? What happened?
   - Do you get *lost* on a daily basis? If so, why?
     - How do the other sheep react to your getting lost all the time?
     - How do the other sheep act toward you when you are found? Do they celebrate each time? Are they angry at you? What feelings do they have?

- What does it feel like to know that Christ has "risked" the other 99 to come find you?
- What does it feel like to know God comes seeking you even though you didn't ask to be found?

3. Imagine yourself now found and placed upon the shoulders of Christ.
   - What does that feel like to be supported in that way? To be carried like that?
   - What does it feel like to have the party thrown for you? Who do you see? What are they saying?
   - What does it sound like to have so many in Heaven rejoicing over you?

4. Imagine yourself as the woman who lost a silver coin.
   - Are you down to your last 10 coins? Are these coins just extra coins that are lying about? How do you feel about them? What do they mean to you?
   - What in your life means a great deal to you that you would turn your entire house over in order to find? Why does it hold that much meaning to you?
   - Imagine that you are the coin and you have been found and rejoiced over. What does that feel like?

5. Imagine yourself fully forgiven by God and rejoiced over.
   - How does that feel?
   - How does it feel to know that sheep and coins can't speak and, therefore, cannot repent and yet God is still extending God's love and mercy?
   - What does it feel like to know that God's mercy comes before our repentance? It is as if God saying, "I forgive you, now within that overwhelming mercy you can repent."
   - Do you have a hard time accepting that God forgives seemingly unforgiveable sins that others commit?
   - Do you have a hard time accepting that God forgives you of sins that you have committed?

6. Imagine yourself as Jesus.

- When have you gone out of your way to find a lost brother or sister? Friend? Loved one? Maybe even an enemy? What was that journey like to go find them? How did they receive you? Was it risky for you?
- Have you ever forgiven someone even when they have not said that they are sorry? How did that feel for you? How did that feel for them?
- Have you ever extravagantly rejoiced over someone who, you feel, most likely did not deserve it? How did it feel to you? How did it feel to them?
- Can you hear the angels in heaven rejoicing over your life?
- If Jesus is the good shepherd who goes to look for the lost sheep, is Jesus also the woman who searches for the lost coin? What would that mean for Christ to fully embrace both his masculine and feminine identity? What would it mean for God to be Father God and Mother God all at the same time?
- What attributes of Jesus from this narrative do you most want to have in your life today? What attributes of Jesus from this narrative do you most want to have in your life ahead?

Write your own story #1

Here is one story where I take a humorous look at the Scripture. This shows how you can take a creative bent to the Scripture if you so choose.

> Luke 15:1-10: [1]"Now the tax collectors and sinners were all gathering around to hear Jesus. [2] But the Pharisees and the teachers of the law muttered, "This man welcomes sinners and eats with them." [3] Then Jesus told them this parable: [4] "Suppose one of you has a hundred sheep and loses one of them. Doesn't he leave the ninety-nine in the open country and go after the lost sheep until he finds it? [5] And when he finds it, he joyfully puts it on his shoulders [6] and goes home. Then he calls his friends and neighbors together and says, 'Rejoice with me; I have found my lost sheep.' [7] I tell you that in the same way there will be more rejoicing in heaven over one sinner who repents than over ninety-nine righteous persons who do not need to repent. [8] "Or suppose a woman has ten silver coins and loses one. Doesn't she light a lamp, sweep the house and search carefully until she finds it? [9] And when she finds it, she calls her friends and neighbors together and says, 'Rejoice with me; I have found my lost coin.' [10] In the same way, I tell you, there is rejoicing in the presence of the angels of God over one sinner who repents."

In our story about the lost sheep and the lost coin, everyone clamors around Jesus to hear what he has to say. The righteous Pharisees show up and see the people from the *wrong side* of the tracks have gathered around Jesus. What is *that* all about? Certainly, the man claiming to be fully divine and fully human – Emmanuel – God with us, would not be hanging around with *those* people. And yet, our dear Pharisees, and I know I am one of them at various times in my life, are mocking and muttering and texting each other – "OMG! (You know, the abbreviation for "Oh, my God!") He is not only welcoming those people he is EATING with them, too!"

I know I am bent on perfectionism. I can see the shortest path in a nanosecond. I can see the better way faster than most. I can tell you what is wrong with something within minutes. I even have an uncanny ability to tell you who is missing out of over a hundred people. I know I am a Pharisee wondering at times what is wrong with certain people and why, oh, why do they constantly find themselves lost!

And yet, truth be told, I am also hopelessly lost. Once when my sister and I were traveling to Delaware for my sister-in-law's bridal shower we went around the DC Beltway twice! Now, this was before the invention of our GPS systems. But REALLLLLLY, it takes a great deal of *talent* to drive around and then AROUND the Beltway. Of course, we just broke down in hilarious laughter – so much so that my dear sister could barely see the road because of the tears of laughter rolling down her cheeks.

I actually hate being lost, too. There is something quite unsettling about it all. I like being in control. I like having my path and sticking to it. I don't like this "let's try this way," "how about down here," or "this path looks like a cool way to go." No. No. No. Follow the yellow arrows. They will keep you safe. Stick to the assigned path.

Yet, Jesus starts talking about this one sheep who is lost. There is one in every flock. These wayward sheep must pave their own way, make their own mistakes, carve out new lands for all to see. And off this one goes. And dear Jesus, who could just stay with the 99 – I mean, 99 is more than enough to tend to, right? –scampers off to find this *one* lost sheep. It really doesn't make a lot of sense to a perfectionist to hear that you would leave 99 well-behaved, following-the-rules, and staying-in-the-lines sheep to find this one sheep who you might never, ever find. I mean, the sheep might be like my sister and I on I-495 somewhere between DC, Maryland, and Virginia. Are you really going to walk alllllllll that way, Jesus?

And yet, for us who are lost, this is music to our ears. "What? You will come find me? No matter where I am? No matter how lost I am? No matter how bad of a pickle I have found myself in? Surely, your grace extends only just soooooo far – is that correct? What did you say, Jesus? Your grace knows no bounds? Your grace and mercy will always come and find me – no matter what? No matter what!?"

And yes, God's grace and mercy will not only come and find us – God will also pick us up – hold us to God's own heart – and then rejoice greatly with a great multitude. For what was lost has been found and will never, ever be lost again.

Write your own story #2

Again, this is a more personal story of someone being *lost* to me but, at moments, *found*. You might want to think about the people in your life who have been lost to you, but they might still be around and you want to locate them. Or, you might want to think about something physically, emotionally, or spiritually that you have lost, that you wish you could regain. And finally, you might want to think about moments when even God felt lost to you.

What I hope that you see is that there are varying levels to us being lost and us being found. As you live into the narrative, allow yourself plenty of width, depth, and breadth in order to go wherever you need to go within the text.

> Luke 15:4-6: Suppose one of you has a hundred sheep and loses one of them. Doesn't he leave the ninety-nine in the open country and go after the lost sheep until he finds it? And when he finds it, he joyfully puts it on his shoulders and goes home. Then he calls his friends and neighbors together and says, 'Rejoice with me; I have found my lost sheep.

Every single day, my sweet mother becomes more and more lost into the fog called dementia or Alzheimer's. What she knew of her past life is no more. Who she knew, she no longer knows. Over the last three years, she has been truly lost to this dreaded disease.

The one exception is that she has been found by one man, her beloved husband. You see, many years ago my mother told me that a man was following her around. I asked her if that man was scary or whether it felt peaceful to have him with her.

She said, "Oh I like him. He is sitting right there." She pointed to an empty chair across the room. "He wants me to dance with him." I responded with tears in my eyes. I knew that my deceased father was still very present with my mother.

"Oh, how lovely, Mom. You know, if he asks you again, you can go on ahead and dance with him. It is okay. You can dance with him forever if you would like."

My mother stared at me and then looked at the figure she saw across the room, "I think I would like that."

I now know from all of my care for people at the end of their lives that my mother was talking in end-of-life language. You see, right now she has "one foot in Heaven and one foot on earth," as I call it. She moves in and out of both realms as she nears her death. She sees people that I cannot see. She hears things that I cannot hear. This does not mean that these people are any less real. For my mother, Daddy is right there with her.

Another interaction or blessing I get to experience with her is what I call *five-second grace moments*. Those are moments that literally last about five seconds where Mom isn't as lost to me; in fact, she is found and very present with me.

One day in Mom's room, I was talking to her caregivers about how my Dad would always tell me: "you only tease those whom you love" and how I would say right back to him "You must REALLY love me!!" I then shared with them, "For instance, my Dad would always ask the minute I would walk into the house after a long 4 ½ hour car drive to come see them, 'So, when are you leaving?'" It was then that my dear Mom, who had been chewing on her chew stick non-stop, put it down and smiled broadly at all of us. It was one of those capricious smiles where you know the person is laughing inwardly. She then picked up her chew stick and started chewing again. We all just burst out in laughter.

Another time, her caregiver was talking about how she had worked two jobs starting at 5:00 AM only to come home at 7:00 PM to two grandchildren and a husband. You can imagine the scene. They were all lying about and asking her, "What's for dinner?"

I then told her caregiver, "Oh, I will never forget the last time my Momma was asked that question by my Daddy. She said, 'What did you say, Tommy? *WHAT* - DID - YOU – SAY - TOMMY? Did you ask what is for dinner, Tommy? Welllllll, I don't know, Tommy? What *is* for dinner, Tommy? You tell me!!'" Right then, my mother who had been doing one of her "pretend sleeping" gigs, opened her eyes, looked around at all of us, and smiled ear to ear. Again, great laughter ensued.

My son Luke took me to see his Granny on Christmas. His Granny yelled at him the last time he saw her, and it upset him so badly that he did not want to return to see her. It was as if she had awakened from a deep sleep just to speak hateful things to him; it was awful. I told him that I wondered if she was hanging on to life because she needed to apologize in her own way to him. Well, she sat there - eyes closed, chewing on her chew stick almost the entire time. But as I would talk about their antics together when Luke was a child, she would smile her wry smile. Luke cried and I cried. Then when he said his final "I love you." She mumbled back which I let him know was her way of saying "I love you, too." It was beautiful and healing for all.

Since that time, Luke has been taking me to see her quite often. He usually cuddles with her as she is sleeping (or pretend-sleeping!) almost the entire time. One time, I played for her on my phone "Just as I am" and "Like a River Glorious" – two of her all-time favorite hymns. I told her a silly story about her mother-in-law, or my Dad's mom, "Mudge," and used my best Mudge voice. For a moment, she giggled using her laugh of olden times.

Another time, I went by to see Mom, and she was more engaged than usual. She kept saying I was "sweet, sweet." And then she looked at me, ran her hand oh so lovingly under my chin, and said "beauty." This little gesture of running her fingers under my chin was something that she did with all of us as children when we were younger. It was one of her gestures of love. And, I certainly felt the amazing love she had for me.

One recent weekend, Luke gave his Granny a kiss and said, "I love you!" to her. She giggled her old giggle. I then leaned in and started kissing her, and she kissed me back time after time after time after time. Of course, she stopped as soon as we wanted to film it! That's my Mom!

But the most poignant story was when I was with my brother Andy. My mother said to us, "No, No, No, No, No, No, No, No, Lost, Lost, Lost, Lost, Lost, Lost..." to which I exclaimed: "Wow Mom, you are no longer lost!" "I, I, I, I, I, I, I, Found, Found, Found, Found, Found, Found ..." to which I replied "Wow, Mom now that you are found, you will never be lost again."

In our Scripture, Jesus asks the question "doesn't he?" versus "does he?" Jesus naturally assumes that you don't just let go of lost sheep even if they are perpetual wanderers who are constantly lost. Jesus always goes looking for the lost ones – the lost memories – the ones lost in the fog. If we are Jesus followers, well then, we are to go looking, too.

Jesus is also telling us to look for those *found* moments or those moments of grace – even if they are only seconds long – in order to be able to rejoice and say, "I have found my lost sheep." And as crazy as it might sound, Jesus thinks it is worth the risk of leaving all of what we know – you know, the 99 - in order to go grab those 5 seconds of grace – those 5 seconds of rejoicing. In this way, we can be and will be Christ for one another.

Write your own sermon for those on the inside

With all of my sermons, you will see, I write them with my friends who are incarcerated in mind. These men and women live in a particular setting that dictates a certain way of life for them. What I hope that I give them is a new light to see the Scripture and how they fit into it.

If you are a pastor, you have your own congregation with their own way of "being together" and their own way of doing things. I think the most powerful sermons are ones where you not only listen intently to what the Spirit is saying about the text, but ones in which you allow yourself to be vulnerable to the text and therefore to your congregation. I think as humans we relate to each other at a deep level when we share our own stories – joys and sorrows, happiness and sadness, all togetherness and brokenness – in the most authentic way we can.

Luke 15:1-10:

> [1] Now the tax collectors and sinners were all gathering around to hear Jesus. [2] But the Pharisees and the teachers of the law muttered, "This man welcomes sinners and eats with them." [3] Then Jesus told them this parable: [4] "Suppose one of you has a hundred sheep and loses one of them. Doesn't he leave the ninety-nine in the open country and go after the lost sheep until he finds it? [5] And when he finds it, he joyfully puts it on his shoulders [6] and goes home. Then he calls his friends and neighbors together and says, 'Rejoice with me; I have found my lost sheep.' [7] I tell you that in the same way there will be more rejoicing in heaven over one sinner who repents than over ninety-nine righteous persons who do not need to repent. [8] "Or suppose a woman has ten silver coins and loses one. Doesn't she light a lamp, sweep the house and search carefully until she finds it? [9] And when she finds it, she calls her friends and neighbors together and says, 'Rejoice with me; I have found my lost coin.' [10] In the same way, I tell you, there is rejoicing in the presence of the angels of God over one sinner who repents."

27

PRAYER: May these feeble words of mine be your words to us and for us. May you enlighten us, revive us, and renew us. May you come and find us in whatever lost country we should find ourselves in. Amen.

Notice the scene: We have all of these people of ill-repute clamoring around Jesus. Jesus does not seem to be the least bit bothered by this fact. I can see him sitting there with the tax collectors, ex-convicts, prostitutes, and other people who seemingly everyone considers to be scum of the earth. All of them are jockeying for position around Jesus to hear what he has to say. The Greek meaning here for "sinner" is one who repeatedly sins – a habitual sinner. These are the worst of the worst in town. These are the "three strikes" people that our society believes should get a life sentence. And yet, gentle Jesus is speaking softly and learning who they are person by person by person because he wants to know each one of them – he wants to know each of their stories.

But we also have the Pharisees and the teachers there, too. These folks who are probably wearing the finest of clothing. These folks who are well versed in the Old Testament. These folks who are steeped in the Levitical Law. These folks who know a law-breaker when they see one. I am sure they are not sitting but standing as they mutter to each other *"This man, this man* welcomes sinners and eats with them. This cannot be the Messiah – the Son of God – Emmanuel – 'God with Us.' If he were, then he would be eating with us and not with '*them.*' The Messiah would know better than to hang out and be stained by the likes of 'those' people. I mean, no Messiah is going to *eat* with a sinner – a habitual offender – a man who constantly finds himself in solitary confinement because even though he is locked behind the walls for all of his misdeeds, he keeps offending; surely, the Messiah can see who these people really are - surely the Messiah understands protocol."

And for our dear writer, Luke, who is jotting this story down, this isn't the first time he is telling us about an encounter between tax collectors, sinners, Pharisees, Scribes, and Jesus. He also writes about them in the 5th chapter when Jesus calls Levi, the tax collector, to be one of his disciples by simply saying the words "follow me" – "follow me" - and Levi follows him. Immediately afterwards, Levi throws a big party – a huge feast. The Pharisees and Scribes get their nose all bent out of shape over that, too. But Jesus reminds them that physicians come only for those who are sick (Luke 5:31).

In our scene, we see that the Pharisees and Scribes are "overhearing" Jesus. But we also see Jesus doing his fair share of overhearing the Pharisees and Scribes. When he hears what they are saying, he pipes up. In his usual style, he tells them a parable or a story and asks a question somewhere in the middle of it. "Suppose one of you has a hundred sheep and loses one of them. Doesn't he leave the ninety-nine in the open country and go after the lost sheep until he finds it?"

As the shepherd, you have 100 sheep to keep track of when one of them goes missing. I am not sure how you know that the one has gone. Don't they all look alike? Don't they all sound about the same? Aren't they all wearing that same khaki outfit? I mean, how do you know? Are you counting "1, 2, 3, 4, 5…" all day long? And doesn't that seem a tad bit tedious? But notice the wording of Jesus' question here. He doesn't ask "does he leave" – no, no, no - he asks "doesn't he leave" – the presumption is, is that this shepherd is going to leave the 99, no questions asked.

Jesus tells us that Jesus knows. Jesus knows when just one sheep is missing. Jesus knows when one is gone. Jesus knows when one voice no longer makes its unique sound. Jesus knows when one who has the tiny spot on its ear is no longer there. Jesus knows, and Jesus without question will go looking. Jesus without question will leave the 99 and will go find the one. The *one*.

Jesus goes on to say: "And when he finds it, he joyfully puts it on his shoulders and goes home. Then he calls his friends and neighbors

together and says, 'Rejoice with me; I have found my lost sheep.'"
Now if you are the lost sheep, you are thinking "Woo hoo, this is
pretty cool. I just walked over miles of rugged terrain only to get
stuck on this really jagged ledge that I thought I was surely going to
fall over when Jesus came to find me. And instead of getting a
switch to the butt, I am getting a free ride on Jesus' shoulders all
the way home. And then as I arrive home I hear everyone
celebrating me! This is the ticket! This is amazing grace – HOW
SWEEEEEEEET the sound!"

If we are honest with ourselves, we can also hear our internal
Pharisee screaming, "You left the 99 to risk your life for that *one*?!
You left the *ninety-nine*?! Jesus, you *know* that one sheep is always
getting lost. Time after time after *unbelievable* time, they find the
paths that are the most dangerous in life and yet you keep risking
your life for *them*?! And you not only go and find them, but you
carry them back home ... *carry them back home*! What is wrong
with you, Jesus! Get a clue! Now, you want all of us to throw a
party?! You want us to celebrate?! This sheep was lost – hopelessly
lost – forever lost – don't you get it?! We call this sheep in the fold
the 'lost one' for a reason!

"Look at us. Look at the 99. We follow all of your rules and
regulations. We follow them so closely every single day that we are
as near perfect as any sheep can be; you know, without blemish
and without flaw. Our parents raised us correctly to follow the rules
every single day in every single way possible. We know the rules so
well that we teach the rules to the other sheep, so they will stay in
line. But this one sheep just doesn't get it – it's hopelessly lost.
Jesus, wake up!"

Don't miss what Jesus says, because it is quite biting to those of us
who are Pharisees or Scribes. "I tell you that in the same way there
will be more rejoicing in heaven over one sinner who repents than
over ninety-nine righteous persons who do not **need** to repent."
You see, we perfect people (Yes, I am one of them.) think that we

are so righteous all the time that we don't need to repent. "What have I done lately? I went to seminary. I study the Bible regularly. I spent two years becoming a Spiritual Director. I delve deeply into the Scriptures day after day. I don't *need* to repent. Not me?! God, you must be talking to someone else." And, Jesus is clear – folks like me – weeeelllll, we won't be rejoiced over in heaven! We are just like the big bunch of 99. We can just go on and stick around the big bunch because clearly we don't – need - Jesus.

Remember, *sinner* here means a habitual sinner, someone who is hopelessly lost in sin. Habitual sinners get how to sin; they just don't understand how to turn around. Well, this is where the sequence of things *really* matters. You see, Jesus does not ask the sheep to first repent and then after that, pick them up. No, no, no; first, Jesus picks up the sheep and puts it ever so gently upon his shoulders.

Watch this: When Jesus grabs us up and puts us on his shoulders, guess what? He turns us around and takes us back home. Do you hear me? When Jesus grabs us and puts us on his shoulders, he turns around and takes us home – to our real home. Jesus is the one who is in the "turn-around" business, who is in the transformation business; we are not! It is only because Jesus can turn us around that we can then repent. It is only in Jesus' showing us the new path that we see we were on the wrong one. It is only because of the extravagant mercy of Jesus, who makes all things new, that we can fully see all that was wrong in our lives.

And maybe as habitual sinners, we might not have the best habits. Jesus showed me after years of suffering with awful insomnia that I don't have a "going to sleep" habit. I just said a "Thank you, God, for the day" kind of a prayer and let that be that. But Jesus showed me, I needed a deeper prayer habit for me and all of my friends behind these prison walls who I hold so dearly all day in prayer. It was not enough for me to merely say "Love you, God" and think I would sleep soundly when I knew that I was carrying all of you and so many other friends on the inside that I care so much about on my heart. So now I have a nightly practice of not only confessing of my sins for the day, but of also bringing forward each of my friend's names to God and giving to God their lives because they are God's anyway.

And Jesus just might want to talk to us about "wandering." We might have wandering eyes – we might watch things on TV that we shouldn't, we might look at things in magazines that we shouldn't, we might look up things on our computers that we shouldn't, we might look at someone in the visitation room in a way that we shouldn't. Whatever it is, we are wandering into lands where we are not supposed to go.

And, this one thing we are doing, we might feel like we need to ask for forgiveness a hundred times but, finally, one day our wandering stops. This is when full repentance happens because, with Jesus' help, we have fully turned it around. Thankfully, Jesus continuously comes to get us. We have changed our path, and we have changed our way. And the marvelous thing is that Heaven rejoices with each of our little steps we make.

Here is something I know about God. Right after the party, God will show you something else to repent of, because we are always becoming perfect. It is about sanctification – about becoming who God intends us to be and about becoming the men and women that God sees us to be. We are not there yet, but in God's eyes we are *becoming* who we are meant to be from the very beginning of time.

After this first parable, we can feel the Pharisee and Scribe tendencies in us. We get itchy when Jesus decides to fling us another story. This time, it is about a woman. A woman who has only 10 silver coins. Well, when she loses the one coin, again, it isn't optional for her to lollygag around and wait for the lost coin to show up. She doesn't have that luxury. She instead lights the lamp, sweeps, cleans, turns things over, looks underneath every piece of furniture, and hunts every dark corner until she finds the one lost coin.

Scripture tells us just like with the lost sheep: "when she finds it, she calls her friends and neighbors together and says, 'Rejoice with me; I have found my lost coin.'" A party is going to happen at 4th and Main Street tonight – a coin that was lost is now found. That coin that can roll into all sorts of dark corners has been found once the light shone on it. That coin that can get buried underneath the dust is no match for a woman and her broom –when God starts sweeping away the cobwebs of our lives.

Jesus ends this parable, "In the same way, I tell you, there is rejoicing in the presence of the angels of God over one sinner who repents." In the parable of the lost sheep, we hear that there will be much rejoicing in Heaven. This time, however, we hear that "the angels of God" are the ones who are going to rejoice. Again, the Greek word is illuminating as these angels are the "heralders of salvation": they announce salvation and they proclaim salvation. Can you imagine that? There are angels in Heaven who have the sole task of shouting unto God "Another one *saved*!" "Another one *saved*!" "Another one let you turn their life around, Jesus!"

I wonder how they do it. Do they use trumpets? Do they use harps? Do they use their voices? And if their voices, do they have really deep voices that carry a long way? Or, do they just scream and shout with soprano voices? I mean, how do they do it? We do not know, but we do know that they are up there screaming and shouting and making quite a racket just because one person repented. *One person*. Not 10. Not 100. *One*.

Have you ever wondered to yourself: Who am I that you are mindful of me, God? (Ps. 8) I am just one person trying to make it in the world. But here is the thing: God rejoices over the *One*. Angels rejoice over the *One*. One person is enough in God's economy to turn Heaven upside down with singing and dancing and totally crazy merriment. Just *One*.

So, will you allow Jesus to put you on his shoulders and turn you around? Will you allow Jesus to take you back home? Will you allow Jesus to show you a better path? A better way? If you are, get ready: There is going to be a WHOLE LOTTA PARTYIN' GOIN' ON just for YOU!

In God's world, God just needs one...

- God needs one man or woman willing to lead the prayer chain for the pod.
- God needs one person on the prison yard to open his Bible and start a Bible study.
- God needs one person to rejoice with a brother or sister when they do even the smallest thing right – when they show they are on the right path.
- God needs one person to sit with a brother or sister just to listen and to be there for them.
- God needs one man or woman to share in brokenness with another – not in a fix-you-up kind of way, but in a "I am here for you, I am broken, too" way.
- God needs one man or woman to seek and find the lost brother or sister who is alone on the yard with no one to talk to.
- God needs one piano player in order to help everyone make a joyful noise during the worship service.
- God says, "You are **my** beloved in whom I am well pleased." Do you know that? Do you really know that?
- God needs one.... to go be Christ....

Will you be that one?

In the name of the Father, the Son, and the Holy Spirit. Amen and Amen.

Write your own Luke 15:1-10 story

Psalm 23

Remember, for your first step, you are just going to get comfortable where you are. Read the Scripture, imagine yourself within the story, and then allow yourself just to *be* with it for 5-10 minutes. You might want to notice words or phrases that catch your eye.

[1] The Lord is my shepherd, I lack nothing.
[2] He makes me lie down in green pastures,
he leads me beside quiet waters,
[3] he refreshes my soul.
He guides me along the right paths
for his name's sake.
[4] Even though I walk
through the darkest valley,
I will fear no evil,
for you are with me;
your rod and your staff,
they comfort me.
[5] You prepare a table before me
in the presence of my enemies.
You anoint my head with oil;
my cup overflows.
[6] Surely your goodness and love will follow me
all the days of my life,
and I will dwell in the house of the Lord
forever.

Phrase by phrase

Now, slow down your reading. Read the psalm phrase by phrase; intentionally read each phrase as if it were the only sentence you are reading. Then move on to the next phrase and again intentionally read that phrase as if it were the only sentence you were reading. Remember to jot notes of what you are feeling or thinking in the blank spaces provided below. Again, reading it twice very slowly is quite helpful.

You might also want to pray a short prayer such as "Gracious God, may your Spirit open my eyes so they may see the truth of the Scripture for me. I want to hear from you. Speak clearly now to me. Amen."

[1] The Lord is my shepherd,

I lack nothing.

[2] He makes me lie down

in green pastures,

he leads me

beside quiet waters,

[3] he refreshes my soul.

He guides me

along the right paths

for his name's sake.

[4] Even though

I walk through

the darkest valley,

I will fear no evil,

for you are with me;

your rod and your staff,

they comfort me.

[5] You prepare a table before me

in the presence of my enemies.

You anoint my head with oil;

my cup overflows.

[6] Surely your goodness and love

will follow me

all the days of my life,

and I will dwell

in the house of the Lord forever.

Questions of the text

Now, we really slow the pace down and examine each phrase. We ask personal questions of each phrase. Remember, focus on only those questions that make your heart skip a beat or make a light go on and you say, "Aha, I get it now" or "What did that just say?" If a question prompts a deeper question, write it down! Also, *welcome* all feelings (negative and positive) as if they were visitors at your front door who you have been longing to see. If you struggle to welcome the feeling, write the feeling down and return to it later when you feel you can welcome it with open arms and an open heart. You also might want to pray to God, "Gracious God, may I hear a word from you about my life – wanted and unwanted, seen and unseen, happy or sad – may your Spirit gently speak as I strive to listen intently to what you would want me to hear."

This time, I am asking questions of each phrase versus asking questions of those in the scene. This is another way to question the text in order to glean a deeper meaning for you.

The LORD is my shepherd,

- When you think of a shepherd, what first comes to your mind?
  - What attributes do you give a shepherd?
  - What does a shepherd look like? Smell like even?
  - How does a shepherd behave?
  - What does a shepherd's day consist of?
- Given these attributes, is the Lord truly "your" shepherd? In what ways is this true day to day?
- Is the Lord truly your sole provider?
- Is the Lord truly your sole protector?
- If the Lord is your shepherd, does that make you a sheep? If so, what are sheep like? Do you think about being herded with the other sheep?
- A typical shepherd can tell the difference between each member of the sheep. A shepherd calls them each by name.

Do you feel like the Lord is that kind of a personal God to you?

I lack nothing.
- Do you really lack nothing? Or, do you feel that you really need something else? If you need something else, what else do you need?
- Do you trust God with all of your needs or only some of them?
- Do you feel like you have to be in control of all aspects of your life or else you will be in lack?
  - Can you hand over control of your entire life to God?
  - What areas of your life are you holding onto because you feel you cannot fully trust God to meet all of your needs?
- Do you understand the difference between a "need" and a "want"?
- When you pray, what are you praying for primarily? Are you praying for God to answer your needs or for God to provide things that you want?
- We are told by Jesus not to worry because God takes care of even the flowers and the birds. Do you have a hard time not worrying about your daily needs?
- What can you do to increase your belief that you lack nothing?

He makes me lie down
- Has there been a time in your life when you have felt that God has *made* you lie down? If so, write that story. You can address the following:
  - What did you feel?
  - Was it a dark period?
  - Did it draw you closer to God?

- o Did it hurt your relationship with God?
- o Did the relationship get better over time?
- How does it feel to hear the words, "he makes me lie down"?
  - o Does this come across as coercive?
  - o Does this sound like God's *shalom*? God's peace? Is God insisting that you rest? Is God insisting that you take a Sabbath rest?

in green pastures,
- How does it feel to realize that God doesn't make you lie down in dirt, but in *green pastures*?
- What do *your* green pastures look like now? What have they looked like in the past? What do you want them to look like?
- Picture yourself lying in the middle of a blossoming field looking up. Maybe you are resting on a blanket or you are having a picnic. The Sun is shining brightly, and the wind seems to be blowing from all directions at once. There isn't another soul in sight – it is just you and your Creator who has said that you are joyfully and wonderfully made.
  - o Describe what else you are able to see.
  - o Describe what else you are able to feel.
  - o Reach out and touch the wild, towering, strains of green grass. Smell the flowers – those yellow daisies. How long have you been there?
  - o How much longer will you stay?

he leads me
- Do you think of God as someone who leads your life? If so, in what ways does God lead your life? If not, *who* leads your life?

- In what areas of your life do you wish that you allowed God to lead more? How can you release these parts of your life to God?
- What keeps you from allowing God to lead *all* areas of your life?
- When God leads you, how does that feel?
    o Does life get better?
    o Does life get worse?
- Why do you think God wants to lead your life?

beside quiet waters,
- How does it feel to hear that God leads you to *quiet* waters?
- Do you need more quiet in your life?
    o If so, how can you make that happen?
    o Do you have meditative practices like centering prayer that work for you?
    o Do you go on retreats where you can sit by a creek and hear the crackle of water?
    o If you live in a clamorous environment, how can you welcome in quiet amidst all of the noise?
- Why do you think that God wants to lead you beside quiet waters?

he refreshes my soul.
- How does it feel to you to know that God "refreshes your soul"?
- In what ways has God done this for you recently?
- What spiritual practices can you do to refresh your soul?

He guides me
- How does it feel for someone to guide you?

- How does *guiding* you differ from *leading* you? Are they different to you? In what ways are they similar? How are they different?
- A typical guide shows you *guideposts* so that you know you are on the right path. In what way has God shown you recently that you are on the right path?
- Why do you think God wants to guide you?

along the right paths
- What does the "right path" mean to you?
- Does the right path mean the *correct* path?
- Is this path a straight line or does it take many twists and turns?
- Have you ever walked a labyrinth?
    - If so, what was it like to make the U-turns?
    - What was it like to totally retrace all of your steps?
    - What did you do when you got to the center of the labyrinth?
- What if the right path is the dark path?

for his name's sake.
- Do you do things for the glory of God?
- Do you praise God for the little things that you are able to do?
- Do you think about the fact that all of the little things in your life are because of God's providence? Because of God's care?

Even though
Ah, these pivotal words! What are you going through right now in your life that is painful or difficult? For example, are you going through a divorce? A separation? Are you having a difficult time with your children? Have friends left you? Are you

unhappy with your job? Is it difficult to decide the next steps in your life?

- Can you put "even though" in front of the painful and difficult things in your life? For example, "even though my son won't speak to me..." "Even though someone significant has died..." "Even though I have a hard time loving myself."?
- How do these two words feel to you?

I walk through the darkest valley,

- What is the darkest valley you have walked through? Write the story.
- What does it feel like to be *walking* vs. crawling, creeping, groveling, dragging, hobbling, or slithering through the darkest valley?
- What happened with your relationship with God?
  - o Did you get closer?
  - o Did you get farther apart?
  - o Did you wonder whether God was even there with you? Do you still wonder?
- Is the darkness of your life always bad? Is it sometimes a good thing? Explain.

I will fear no evil,

- How much does fear dictate what you do and not do?
- What would it mean to your life to say, "I will fear nothing"? How would that feel to not fear anything?
- Do you feel like you always have victory over evil even before you confront it? Or, do you feel like evil has victory over you so you better not confront it? Explain.

for you are with me;

- We are told repeatedly in the Old Testament and New Testament that God will never leave us nor forsake us. Do you believe this? If so, how does that feel to you? If not, what does that feel like to feel abandoned by God?

- Do you believe God is with you in the dark?
- Do you believe God is with you during your worst days or just during your best days? If just during your best days, what does it feel like to know that God is with you in your darkest days?

your rod and your staff,

- When you hear "rod" and "staff," what comes to mind? Have you ever had a negative experience with either? If so, tell the story.
- Remembering that God is our *shepherd*, does this change what you think of "rod" and "staff"?

they comfort me.

- God's rod and staff bring comfort. How can they do that in your life?
- Would this transform the way you think about "rod" and "staff"?

You prepare a table before me

- What does the table look like? How long is it? How ornate is it? How plain is it?
- What has God put on top of the table?
- A table is flat and even. Do you feel like when you reach the table that you have made it through the darkness to something more safe and secure? Do you feel like you can rest here, finally, from your travels? From your journey of twists and turns?
- A table is something stable to put your most precious things on top of – what would you put on your table? What is most precious to you?

in the presence of my enemies.

- Does it surprise you that the table is set in front of your enemies versus your friends?
- Why would God set the table in front of your enemies?
  - What is God trying to teach you?
  - What is God trying to teach them?
- Have you ever tried to reconcile with someone who has betrayed you? Someone who has harmed you? What was that like? What was it like to share a meal with them afterward?

You anoint my head with oil;

- Has anyone anointed your head with oil? If so, share that story.
- If no one has anointed your head with oil, what do you think that would feel like?
- Why does God think it important to anoint your head with oil? What is the oil's significance?

my cup overflows.

- Have you had an experience where you felt like your cup was *overflowing*? What was that like? What did it feel like? Tell the story.
- Describe a cup.
  - What are its attributes?
  - How can you be more like a cup?

Surely your goodness and love

- What does the word "surely" mean to you? Have you ever experienced something or someone or even God as a "surely"?
- What does God's goodness feel like?
- What does God's love feel like?

- How does it feel that we can be assured of God's goodness and love?
- God has not stopped pursuing us. God never will. How does that make you feel?
- How do you think God feels when we take time to acknowledge God's goodness?

will follow me
- How does it feel to have someone or something follow you?
- How does it feel to know that "surely" God's *goodness* will follow you?
- How does it feel to know that "surely" God's *love* will follow you?
- How does God's goodness and love follow you on a day to day basis? What does that look like in reality?
- What or who has God used lately to chase you down?

all the days of my life,
God is talking about *all* the days of your life. Does it feel like God is with you every single day?
- Describe the days where you feel God close by.
- Describe the days where you do not feel God at all.
- What is different about these two types of days?

and I will dwell
- *Dwell* in Hebrew means to inhabit, remain, or abide. Which definition resonates most with you and your life right now? Why?
- How does it feel to know that you *will* dwell – you *will* remain – you *will* abide with God?

in the house of the LORD forever.

- The *house* in Hebrew could mean "in the household" or "in the family" of God. How does that feel to you?
- "In the household" or "in the family" of God. Do they feel differently to you?
- How does it feel to know you will be in the house of the Lord forever?
- What is your concept of Heaven? What do you think will happen after you die?
- Do you think your house will look different than other people's? If so, how will your house be different? What will their houses look like?

Write your own story #1

Now, write your own story using the Psalm 23 story. This might feel daunting at first. You might be asking questions: What kind of story? What should I say? How long should it be? There are no right or wrong answers to these questions. It should be as long or as short as you need it to be. These are your stories and whatever you write will be perfect for you.

This is one example of something that I wrote for Psalm 23. It is a short devotion that I believe packs a lot in it. This is a perfect example of something that you could use for a Spiritual Direction group which I describe in "Appendix C. Using this book in a spiritual direction group." (page 170)

> Psalm 23: The Lord is my shepherd, I lack nothing.
> He makes me lie down in green pastures,
> he leads me beside quiet waters,
> he refreshes my soul.
> He guides me along the right paths
>   for his name's sake.
> Even though I walk
>   through the darkest valley,
> I will fear no evil,
>   for you are with me;
> your rod and your staff,
>   they comfort me.
> You prepare a table before me
>   in the presence of my enemies.
> You anoint my head with oil;
>   my cup overflows.
> Surely your goodness and love will follow me
>   all the days of my life,
> and I will dwell in the house of the Lord
>   forever.

When I go to Death Row, there are times when I have to wait. And when I mean wait, I mean **wait**. The prison staff tells me, "it will be

50

soon." But they never define *soon*. *Soon* could be 10 minutes, or it could be 30 minutes or longer. And so, my practice is to read a Psalm over and over and over again until it really sinks into my soul.

This one particular day, I was feeling antsy all over and I was trying to present a façade of peace and calm. I started to read Psalm 23. I usually focus on "he maketh me lie down" because of my various health issues that have caused me to have to lie down and rest. This week, the words that seemed to be printed in bold and enlarged font were "even though." *Even though*.

I love Scripture. I love the writers of Scripture. You see, they throw in little phrases like *even though* that turn Scripture on its head. You are lollygagging through life when all of the sudden life takes many twists and turns that you don't want life to take and these words, *even though,* show up. God then says to you, *even though* you should walk through your deepest and darkest valley, errr hmmm, do not fear ... and especially don't fear evil. *Even though* those around you are causing you massive heartache and heartbreak, I am with you. *Even though* all you can see is the dark and you wonder if it will ever be light again, do not be afraid – nope – don't do it, because I am there to comfort you. *Even though* you are going through a very difficult time and you wonder where I went, keep walking. Remain upright because that shows everyone else that "I am" with you.

If all of this seems completely nonsensical to you, then join the rest of us. As I let it wash over me as pure grace, I realize how astounding all of this is. These two words, *even though*, pack a powerful punch and assure me of the presence of our God who loves us endlessly.

As I started to think about my friends on the inside and their *even though*s, I thought: *Even though* I am walking through my darkest days – *even though* I am surrounded by the depth of darkness and dankness – *even though* I smell only the dirt of living underground – *even though* no one comes to visit me – *even though* my friends and family have turned away from me – *even though* I have been betrayed by person after person – *even though* I just want to barricade myself in my cell and never come out - *even though* – *even though* – God is still present. God is still here. God is still there holding us and loving us. And, so we can indeed walk. We can walk into the deepest and darkest of nights knowing God *is* with us.

Write your own story #2

This is an example of something I wrote where I used just a phrase from Psalm 23. Sometimes, just one little phrase makes your heart thump loudly or causes your breath to gasp. Scripture has a way of catching us and making us wonder whether we have ever read *that* Scripture before even though it seems like the Scripture in our mind is a well-worn path. So, let Scripture surprise you. Be open to it speaking as if it had never spoken before to you. Let the Spirit speak!

As you will soon see, this story and the last story are very different. By slowing down and reading the Scripture at a slower pace, it allowed me to see the Scripture with new eyes. And then, I could wear new glasses to see how that Scripture applied to me and to my life. Yes, *even though* I might be going through a difficult time, I am still walking. And even if God "maketh me lie down," I know the next time around, I will be resting in God's arms.

Psalm 23:2: "He maketh me lie down…"

One of my interns brought this Scripture, "He maketh me lie down," to our theological reflection time at the beginning of 2014. She exclaimed, "it isn't very nice of God. In fact, God comes off sounding pretty harsh, don't ya' think?" I started to belly laugh as I had never read this short little phrase with such an undertone. But it was right there – staring at me – you know, like **all** the time – but I hadn't seen it. This Psalm that I have read countless times, especially with all of my work with the dying and the bereaved, was saying God **maketh** me. And I thought it was being so nice and gentile!

When I started 2014, I had already lost 20 or so pounds, and I was flat out exhausted. I had found out in December that my mononucleosis had returned. If you have had mono twice in your teens, you will get mono again when you are in your 50s (and older) if you are under too much stress. It *reactivates* itself in your system.

53

So, you have to learn to live a peace-filled life unless you want to sleep through the last half of your existence!

The major reason I had lost so much weight was I could not eat anything. And I mean I could **not** eat anything. I would eat a half a cup of food and feel like it was all going to come back up. Thank God for banana shakes with protein powder in them or else I would have surely wasted away.

The doctors and surgeons soon discovered the issue going on in my body and told me to "prep" for surgery. Let me just tell you now, if you walk into surgery this weak and this tired, you are setting yourself up for a **very** long recovery time. I truly felt like I was a baby back in her mother's arms as I had to turn over all of the caretaking of my body to those around me. I could do *nothing* by myself. Well, I could sleep! And sleep I did for months, it seemed. If a person can hibernate, I hibernated!

Throughout, God reminded me again and again and again of this Scripture, "he maketh me lie down..." (Ps 23:2). It goes on to say "green pastures." However, I struggled to always see the green pastures especially because during this time I felt I needed to walk away from my job. All I saw was a lot of dirt in my eyes, my eyelashes, my nose, my ears, and my fingernails. I still kept the faith that the dirt would not have the final word and just laid down and rested there – you know - in the dirt – in the dusty, musty dirt.

Then, it became obvious that something had gone wrong with my surgery as a bulge in my stomach just would not go away. I finally saw my doctor who told me that I would need hernia surgery. I really wanted to scream and cry.

So, my dear Scripture "He maketh me lie down..." (Ps. 23:2) remained with me. My recovery time was once again very slow. And, I learned anew what it meant to rest in God. My image for the year became a child who crawls into their mother's lap and is just held there. There is safety there. There is Love. You can hear God's own heartbeat there. You just have to slow down, lie down, steady your own heartbeat, lean in, fully rest, and then intently listen ... you will hear it. It is a gentle, rhythmic, soothing thumping. This **is** a place you can really rest as you are totally held by the one who loves you the most. Maybe these are the greenest of pastures after all....

Write your own sermon for those on the inside

After all of the reflection that I did on Psalm 23 (literally more than a year), I wrote this sermon for my friends on the inside. Notice how I step them through each phrase, so they can hopefully see the Scripture in a new way. These men are my friends, so I felt that I could speak to their situation and to what I thought their hearts long for the most. Also, notice how I use one of my saddest days as a thread throughout the sermon.

> Psalm 23:
> The Lord is my shepherd, I lack nothing.
> He makes me lie down in green pastures,
> he leads me beside quiet waters,
>   he refreshes my soul.
> He guides me along the right paths
>   for his name's sake.
> Even though I walk
>   through the darkest valley,
> I will fear no evil,
>   for you are with me;
> your rod and your staff,
>   they comfort me.
> You prepare a table before me
>   in the presence of my enemies.
> You anoint my head with oil;
>   my cup overflows.
> Surely your goodness and love will follow me
>   all the days of my life,
> and I will dwell in the house of the Lord
>   forever.

Prayer: Gracious God, use these feeble words of mine to be your words. May you give them life beyond just words on a page. May you make them live, move, and breathe in order to give us new life – in order to give us a new way of seeing you. May you transform our hearts and thereby our lives and may we never be the same. Amen.

Ah, our old familiar text. "The Lord is my shepherd." Yes, the Lord *is* my shepherd. I am just one of his many sheep. And if the truth be known, I am probably the one that goes wandering off without much thought to where the rest of the flock is heading. But the shepherd, always with a laugh and a smile, comes to find me time and time again, puts me on his shoulders, and carries me back to the rest of the flock. The shepherd knows that I love to take advantage of this moment, as I whisper into his ear all that is going on in my life.

"I lack nothing." I want for nothing. Years ago, I thought I needed so much. But now that I am in ministry, I have realized that I lack nothing. I have all I need when I have God. God is the provider and sustainer of my life. I lack nothing.

But then, this psalm that I have recited a thousand times in an almost catatonic state was totally upended one day when one of my interns brought the next line of the Scripture to our theological reflection time. "He maketh me lie down..." She exclaimed, "It isn't very nice of God. In fact, God comes off sounding pretty harsh, don't ya' think?" I started to belly laugh as I had never read this short little phrase with such an undertone.

But it was right there, staring at me; I hadn't seen it. This psalm that I have read countless times, especially with all of my work with the dying and the bereaved, even here on the hospice wards, was saying "God **maketh** me lie down." And I thought this psalm was being so nice and gentile!

It was actually during that time that God was "making **me** lie down" on one surgery table after another in order to get the medical care that I needed. So, this one line became for me words that I dwelled on day after day after day for almost a year.

This line also became very real for me when one of the men on death row was executed just a few weeks ago. But I want us to read the whole line: "He makes me lie down in green pastures... He makes me lie down in green pastures." This beloved man was led to a gurney and told to lie down so that various IVs could be stuck in his arm so that we could execute him and pronounce him dead by 9:17 PM by lethal injection.

Now, I don't want us to get our theology wrong here. God did not make his beloved son lie down on the gurney. Our God is a God who makes us lie down only in green pastures. God does not make us lie down in commensurate pastures. Our God makes us lie down in green pastures – grace-filled pastures. If man creates for us hate-filled pastures, God create for us grace-filled pastures – green pastures.

"He leadeth me…" God is gently showing me the way. God is not coercing me, God is leading me. And to where? To quiet waters. To stilllllllll waters.

Ahhhhh close your eyes for a minute and imagine that you are sitting on a wooden bench beside a creek. You hear the rustle and the crackling of the water breaking over the rocks. As you breathe in and breathe out, you feel a peace that consumes you.

"He leadeth me besides quiet waters." (Wait a few minutes.)

"He refreshes my soul." God knows that your soul takes in so much pain and grief. And, God wants you to know that God is in the *refreshing* business or in the restoration business. God can hold your pain and grief and make you whole again.

"He guides me." God is guiding us… God is guiding me. Where to this time? Along the right paths for his name's sake. We are led to know the right paths that our lives should take – the right way to live our lives – all so that we can give glory to God by the life that we lead. Each of us has a purpose here on earth whether we are inside or outside these walls. It does not matter – God still leads us along the right paths so that our purpose will be clear and so God's name will be glorified.

"Even though." "Even though I walk through the darkest valley..." The psalmist brings this up for us as the worst-case scenario – the darkest valley which we know is death. And in so doing, the psalmist almost begs us to insert our own life event into the psalm. The psalmist begs us to state our own "even though."

Even though I am grieving,
even though I am struggling with health issues,
even though I am struggling to see God in the huge mess I have made,
even though no one is visiting me,
even though family and friends have left me,
even though I feel like I am all alone on the yard,
even though the other men taunt me in the pod,
even though I don't hear God right now,
even though I don't feel like God is answering my prayers,
even though all I see is darkness,
even though I am grieving the death of my parent who I was unable to see before they died,
even though I am praying intently for my sister who has stage 4 lung cancer,
even though...
even though...
whatever YOUR "even though" is...
the psalmist says, "I will walk. I will fear no evil."

I have many friends who tell me, "I have been **through** it!" And, you know what they mean by that. They feel as though they have been tossed from side to side. The ground they are standing on is not what we would call *terra firma* or firm ground; it is more like quicksand. Roaring overhead is Hurricane Patricia – a category 5 coming through!"

And yet, and yet, they keep on walking... they aren't crawling, they aren't creeping, they aren't dragging themselves, they aren't hobbling or slithering, they aren't groveling, they aren't sauntering,

59

they aren't ambling, they aren't scraping by, they aren't even *two-steppin'* it - they are walking... they are **walking**... It is a faith *walk*, not a faith crawl! A faith walk!

Because they can say with complete confidence, "I will fear no evil…" And how can the psalmist say that? Because, "thou art with me."

The psalmist knows that they know that they know that they know because they have been "through it" time and time again. God has not taken the last train to Santa Fe – nay, nay. God is still standing right there. God did not abandon them; God did not leave them. God remained through the storm – through the suffering. I don't have **anything** to fear, including evil, including the darkest valley, including death.

"Your rod and your staff they comfort me." I don't know if these objects conjure up in your mind objects that were used to whip your beeeehind when you were younger, but that's what comes to my mind. Again, God is saying, "In my hands, things that might otherwise be used to harm are used to protect, to lead, to guide, and to comfort because I love you; you are mine."

"You prepare a table before me." God has always been in the radical hospitality business. God is always throwing the party like we see in the story of the prodigal son who comes home. We serve a God who is rich in mercy and grace. I love to repeat the words from Bob Ekblad's book, *Reading the Bible with the Damned*, as one of the men in Bob's Bible study opened up Scripture for me: "I thank God that God is a God of great grace. It was God who handed to Moses, the murderer, the stone tablets that said "thou shalt not murder." God did not strike him down. God instead showed Moses God's glory."[1]

---

[1] Ekblad, Bob, *Reading the Bible with the Damned*, Louisville, KY. Westminster John Knox Press, 2005, 108-110. Note that this is my paraphrase of what the guys said to Bob.

So, we should not be surprised that this long table of luscious food and beverage is set out "in the presence of my enemies." For many years, I have thought of this as almost a "Ha, ha! I am better than you" kind of thing. Now, I don't think so; I think God wants us to finally reconcile. If we don't have reconciliation this side of Heaven, God wants us to find it **in** Heaven. So, this table will be set in one place or the other. It is really our choice as to where it will be.

"You anoint my head with oil;" God is also always in the sanctifying business. God always wants us to see that even the most ordinary moments of our lives are sacred and are to be treated as such. If we do this, look what happens. "My cup overflows." My cup overflows! There is so much goodness and love that our cups will overflow. And they overflow not for us but for all of those who are around us. God wants us to be vessels of God's love and light and so God wants us to overflow – **overflow** with love in order to touch other people's lives.

And now another stop-worthy word: "Surely," "Surely." Most certainly – you can bet your last dollar on it – you can know it to be absolutely the truth – but what is the absolute truth? There are two absolute truths here, so let's lean in and get them both.

"Surely your goodness and love will follow me all the days of my life…." I don't know if you have ever had the experience of someone stalking you. Thankfully, God's stalking is the good kind of stalking. God's stalking says that both God's goodness and God's love will follow me all the days of my life.

God's goodness will surround me.

God's love will track me down.

God's love will find me.

God's love will not leave me alone.

God's goodness and love will follow me all the days of my life."

And secondly, "and **surely** I will dwell in the house of the LORD forever." I **will** dwell. I **will** dwell. Not I *may* dwell if I do this or that. I **will** dwell in the house of the Lord forever.

It is that blessed assurance we hoped for and depended on as I stood vigil outside the prison in Virginia with about 10 other people on that very blustery and rainy night.

As one of the fellow vigil members held a flashlight, I started to read Psalm 23. A hush came over the little group and they formed a circle around me.

After I finished reading, a woman standing next to me piped up and said "Thank you. I am his sister."

I hugged her and held her close. "Can I read something else?"

"John 14?"

"Yes." I read the Scripture for all to hear that the Father's home in Heaven has many rooms.

I then asked the small crowd if it would be okay if I prayed. They all agreed.

I prayed as one of my Duke Divinity professors, Dr. Turner, had taught me: "Pray what you know... pray what you know."

"Gracious God, there are no words. The grief is too much. Our hearts are breaking... surely, your heart is breaking, too, oh God... you weep, too. God... you hold our tears. Thank you for your beloved son and for his life and that you don't define him by his crime but rather as your beloved son in whom you are well pleased."

There was not a dry eye. I held his sister still close by my side. We all just stared at that awful prison. We were all speechless.

And so at 9:17 PM, he died. "And I **will** dwell in the house of the Lord forever." Yes, God's beloved son, surely you will. Surely you will.

Our God is a God who is with us **in** our greatest suffering. God is still our God who will never leave us nor forsake us.

Our God is relentless in God's pursuit of each and every one of us because of God's great love for us. I thank God that we are **not** defined by our worst sin. Rather, we are defined by God's unrelenting, uncompromising, unconditional love for us.

God is always there, wooing us and loving us. But we have to lean in – listen – and respond.

God's way is the way of peace. God's way is the way of cups overflowing... God's way is the way of goodness... God's way is the way of restoration... God's way is the way of love.

May we walk each and every day – being led by God's love – in order to love those around us - until we meet God face to face.

May it be so. May it be so. Amen and Amen!

Write your own Psalm 23 story

John 20:11-18

At first, just read the text. Try to live inside it. Who is there? Who isn't there? Try to *be* with the Scripture. Try to hear it as if you are hearing it for the first time. I think, especially with the Easter story, that we rush to the risen Christ and yet what we need to do is to deeply listen for what comes before Christ's rising. Try to imagine what feelings and emotions that Mary Magdalene is experiencing as she runs to the tomb. Think about where she has been over the last three days and what she must have felt with all of those steps that came before. Just be with your emotions as if you were Mary.

[11] But Mary stood weeping outside the tomb. As she wept, she bent over to look into the tomb; [12] and she saw two angels in white, sitting where the body of Jesus had been lying, one at the head and the other at the feet. [13] They said to her, "Woman, why are you weeping?" She said to them, "They have taken away my Lord, and I do not know where they have laid him." [14] When she had said this, she turned around and saw Jesus standing there, but she did not know that it was Jesus. [15] Jesus said to her, "Woman, why are you weeping? Whom are you looking for?" Supposing him to be the gardener, she said to him, "Sir, if you have carried him away, tell me where you have laid him, and I will take him away." [16] Jesus said to her, "Mary!" She turned and said to him in Hebrew, "Rabbouni!" (which means Teacher). [17] Jesus said to her, "Do not hold on to me, because I have not yet ascended to the Father. But go to my brothers and say to them, 'I am ascending to my Father and your Father, to my God and your God.'" [18] Mary Magdalene went and announced to the disciples, "I have seen the Lord"; and she told them that he had said these things to her.

Phrase by phrase

Now let's slow down our reading by going phrase by phrase. Read each phrase with great intentionality before moving onto the next phrase. Feel the emotions. Welcome sad emotions as well as happy emotions. Stop when you need to and breathe in and breathe out. Say a prayer of welcoming for all feelings as feelings of grace which are there to shed light on who you are. Again, write down any emotion, feeling, question, or thought that you might have of the text as you read each phrase as if it was the only phrase you had to read.

[11] But Mary stood weeping

outside the tomb.

As she wept,

she bent over to look into the tomb;

[12] and she saw two angels in white,

sitting where the body of Jesus

had been lying,

one at the head

and the other at the feet.

[13] They said to her, "Woman, why are you weeping?"

She said to them, "They have taken away my Lord,

and I do not know where they have laid him."

[14] When she had said this, she turned around

and saw Jesus standing there,

but she did not know that it was Jesus.

[15] Jesus said to her, "Woman, why are you weeping?

Whom are you looking for?"

Supposing him to be the gardener,

she said to him, "Sir, if you have carried him away,

tell me where you have laid him,

and I will take him away."

[16] Jesus said to her, "Mary!"

She turned

and said to him in Hebrew, "Rabbouni!"

(which means Teacher).

[17] Jesus said to her, "Do not hold on to me,

because I have not yet ascended to the Father.

But go to my brothers

and say to them, 'I am ascending to my Father

and your Father, to my God and your God.'"

[18] Mary Magdalene went

and announced to the disciples,

"I have seen the Lord";

and she told them

that he had said these things to her.

Questions of the text

Take another deep breath in and out. Now, read the Scripture again one more time. But this time, instead of going phrase by phrase, I will ask you questions for each major part of the story. This is another way you can ask yourself questions of the text instead of going phrase by phrase. Sometimes looking at each scene as its own "act" within the overall "play," you can see things about the text that you have not seen before.

In this set of questions, I ask you what it is like to be Christ. You might want to identify with Christ to see how you could be more Christ-like in your day to day interactions.

> [11] But Mary stood weeping outside the tomb. As she wept, she bent over to look into the tomb; [12] and she saw two angels in white, sitting where the body of Jesus had been lying, one at the head and the other at the feet. [13] They said to her, "Woman, why are you weeping?" She said to them, "They have taken away my Lord, and I do not know where they have laid him." [14] When she had said this, she turned around and saw Jesus standing there, but she did not know that it was Jesus. [15] Jesus said to her, "Woman, why are you weeping? Whom are you looking for?" Supposing him to be the gardener, she said to him, "Sir, if you have carried him away, tell me where you have laid him, and I will take him away." [16] Jesus said to her, "Mary!" She turned and said to him in Hebrew, "Rabbouni!" (which means Teacher). [17] Jesus said to her, "Do not hold on to me, because I have not yet ascended to the Father. But go to my brothers and say to them, 'I am ascending to my Father and your Father, to my God and your God.'" [18] Mary Magdalene went and announced to the disciples, "I have seen the Lord"; and she told them that he had said these things to her.

1. Imagine yourself in the scene.

    John 20:1 states: "while it was still dark." In other words, this scene plays out while it is still dark outside.

    - What is it like to be outside the tomb of Jesus when it is still dark outside?

- Did you bring a torch with you?
- What is it like to see the huge stone rolled away?
- What is it like to see Jesus missing?
- You have been grieving – how long has that gone on? How has that felt?
- How long has it been since you slept?
- Are you trusting what you are seeing? Feeling?
- How much strength do you have?
- When was the last time you have eaten anything?

2. Imagine that you are Mary *at the tomb*.
   - The Scripture starts by saying, "But Mary." Has there been a time when everyone else was heading one way, but you decided a different path? What was that like for you? Were you tempted to go the way everyone else was going? Or, were you steadfast in the path that you took?
   - You are on the "outside." Has there been a time when you are on the outside looking in? What was that like for you?
   - You are already weeping as you stand outside the tomb. Then, you look in and see just the two angels. Do you think they are just mirages? Do you believe they are real angels? Do you want to run? Do you want to stay? Are you afraid? Do they bring you comfort? Why do you think they are initially there? What are your first thoughts?
   - You tell the angels, "They have taken away my Lord, and I do not know where they have laid him."

     - Have you ever been this frightened?
     - Has a loved one gone missing in your life? What did you feel? What did you do? Were you even able to breathe?

71

- How do you personally answer them, "Woman (man), why are you weeping?" Have you had a dark time in your life when friends have shown up and asked you, "Why are you weeping?" How did you answer them? Did they understand your holy tears?
- Are there times when you feel like Christ is missing in your life? Have you gone searching for him, only to discover that he is not there? If so, what does that feel like?

3. Imagine that you are Mary confronted *now with Jesus*.
   - You turn around from seeing an empty tomb, and you are weeping. What are you feeling? Are you seeing clearly? Are you feeling weak? Are you even perhaps hungry or thirsty without realizing it?
     - What is stirring within you?
     - Have you ever grieved for a long period of time? What was that like for you? Tell the story.

   - Jesus himself asks you the same question, "Woman (man), why are you weeping?" How do you answer him? Can you remember a dark time in your life when Christ asked you this question? Did you answer him sarcastically? Or, are you so drained with grief that you just cannot respond at all?
   - How do you answer Jesus' next question, "Whom are you looking for?"
     - What kind of Jesus do you need to show up for you? What are his attributes?
     - What kind of Jesus did you need when you lost a very close friend? Family member?

   - You at first think he is the gardener. What do you do when someone you know is in front of you, but you cannot place them? What was happening in your life that made you feel this way?

- You say, "Sir, if you have carried him away, tell me where you have laid him, and I will take him away."
  - Have you ever desperately wanted Jesus back?
  - What would you have said or done to get him back?
  - Are you screaming and crying? Or, are you calm and collected?

- Imagine right now that it is you standing in front of Jesus in front of that empty tomb while it is still dark. Jesus says your name. Hear your name said over and over again by Jesus.
  - What does it feel like to have Jesus personally say your name? How does Jesus say it? What tone is he using?
  - What does his face look like as he says it?

- What is it like to realize that Jesus was with you the whole time in your darkness?
  - Was it difficult to know Jesus was there in the dark with you just being silent?
  - What is it like to recognize him *as if for the first time*?

- Mary calls Jesus "teacher." Why would she pick this one particular attribute or role? Do you think of Jesus as a teacher? In what ways?
  - Would you have called him "teacher," too? If not, what name / attribute would you have used?

- Jesus tells you, "Do not hold on to me, because I have not yet ascended to the Father." How difficult would this be for you right now? If a loved one (mother, father, sister, brother, or friend) came back to life even for 10 minutes, what would be your first instinct?

- What does it feel like for Jesus to tell you, a woman, to "go" and herald the news that Christ has risen? (Remember, women were basically nobodies at that time!)
  - Has Christ called you to tell others about him and you felt like you were a "nobody" and that you were unqualified to tell others? Does this keep you away from your calling?
  - Have you ever been one of the world's "nobodies"? How did that feel? How did that happen? Tell your story.
  - Yet, Jesus transforms this woman into one of the world's greatest "somebodies." Have you been through that transformation? What was that like? Tell your story.

- Jesus tells you: "'I am ascending to my Father and your Father, to my God and your God.'" What does the use of "my" and "your" pronouns say to you? How do those words make you feel?
- How does it feel to tell the room of "qualified people" that you have "seen the Lord!"?
  - What is it like to share your testimony? What do you share? What do you say that Christ told you?
  - If you are a woman who has lived into your calling as a pastor and minister, have you been met with resistance? If so, what was that like? How did that feel? How does it feel that Jesus has called you to be the first person to tell the very good news that Christ is alive?

- You started the day as a grieving woman who lost the most important person in her life. However, you are ending your day as a heralder of the very good news that Jesus has risen. How are you feeling? Have you ever had a day filled with the lowest of lows as well as the highest of highs? Describe.
- What do you understand are the implications of a risen Jesus? What are you telling the disciples that this means?
  - What does a "risen" Jesus mean to your life now?
  - What do you say to others who ask you about the resurrection?

4. Imagine that you are one of the disciples.
   - Two disciples, Peter and "the other disciple," had already run into the tomb and witnessed for themselves that it was empty. We are told "the other disciple" believed and the two of them ran back.
     - What did "the other disciple" believe?
     - Why are the disciples running away?
     - Have you ever been so overwhelmed by a situation that you ran away? What happened?
     - Did you believe something in your head, but your heart had a hard time taking it in?
   - Where are the other 10 disciples? Are they catatonic with the enormity of their grief? Or, are they able to move around and take care of the business at hand?
   - What is it like to hear the prophetic proclamation, "I have seen the Lord," from a marginalized woman?

- What is it like to hear the very good news from the last person you would expect to hear it from?
- Have you ever been confronted by hearing a truth in your life from a person who others counted out, but Jesus called? If so, what was that like?
5. Now imagine that you are Christ.
   - You have just risen from the dead. What does that feel like?
     - When we are baptized, we too are called to die with Christ and then be raised to new life. What was that experience like for you? Did you hear the words from God that Jesus heard "You are my beloved in whom I am well pleased"?
     - What does it mean to be transformed? To have a new life?
   - What can you learn from Christ here about what you should do when you are with someone who is grieving?
   - How can we learn from the fact that Christ is asking Mary questions about her grief before he reveals to her that he is the risen Christ?
   - As Jesus, you are announcing to a woman, and not a man, the good news that you have been raised from the dead. How does that shape your thoughts on how Jesus viewed women? How does that shape your thoughts on women in ministry?
   - What attributes of Jesus do you most want to have in your life today? In your life ahead?

Write your own story #1

In this story, I interact with Jesus as if I am actually Mary Magdalene at the tomb. By play-acting the character of Mary, it opened my eyes to the Scripture text and to those around Jesus. By putting myself into the role, I try to bring out Mary's feelings by living in her shoes – walking around in them – in order to see, feel, and hear what she is experiencing.

> John 20:11-18: "But Mary stood weeping outside the tomb. As she wept, she bent over to look into the tomb; and she saw two angels in white, sitting where the body of Jesus had been lying, one at the head and the other at the feet. They said to her, "Woman, why are you weeping?" She said to them, "They have taken away my Lord, and I do not know where they have laid him." When she had said this, she turned around and saw Jesus standing there, but she did not know that it was Jesus. Jesus said to her, "Woman, why are you weeping? Whom are you looking for?" Supposing him to be the gardener, she said to him, "Sir, if you have carried him away, tell me where you have laid him, and I will take him away." Jesus said to her, "Mary!" She turned and said to him in Hebrew, "Rabbouni!" (which means Teacher). Jesus said to her, "Do not hold on to me, because I have not yet ascended to the Father. But go to my brothers and say to them, 'I am ascending to my Father and your Father, to my God and your God.'" Mary Magdalene went and announced to the disciples, "I have seen the Lord"; and she told them that he had said these things to her."

I continue to sit in the dark – waiting – constantly waiting for Jesus to appear. You know that "liminal space" where you feel you are just on the threshold of something big happening, but all around you is dirt, wilderness, and darkness. Tears have been streaming from my eyes; they are not wiped away. The tears remain on my face, and I deeply breathe in the saltiness of them. My tears define me.

Before the light of day even dawns, I stand in front of an empty tomb and hear, "Woman why are you weeping?" I guess I am seeing angels, but my mind may be playing tricks on me. Why don't they use my name, Mary?

And why are they asking, "'Why am I weeping?' Seriously!? Are you asking me that in a serious tone? Have you hung around me at all? Do you *really* want me to tell you about the enormity of my grief? Do you want me to share with you how life all of the sudden got so tragic?" I have no energy within me to answer their question, therefore I just ask them to point the way to where Jesus' body is.

I realize the only thing for me to do is to turn around and go look for Jesus. Oh how my body is betraying me. I am dehydrated from days of great grief. My legs are cramping and my side is aching. I am still sobbing. I turn and I barely look up. I see a man in front of me, but I can't make out his face because of all of my tears.

"Woman, why are you weeping? Whom are you looking for?" What is it with this question of why I am weeping? I need my Jesus! I need him now! My mouth is so dry I fumble with my words. "Please, I beg of you to tell me where Jesus is! Do you know where the others have taken him? My grief is insurmountable I need someone to understand how my life all of the sudden went dark."

"I might know something about that."

"What do you know? You are a gardener! You have been tending to these bushes and these flowers? What do you know about all that I have seen, heard, and felt? What do you know about sitting in the darkness of your grief only to feel like it will never be day again?"

"It all went dark when I screamed 'Why?'"

"What are you talking about? What did you do, scream 'why,' and then run into one of these tombs? Why would you do such a thing? I think that I can handle my grief some days and other days, I just want to end it all as it just gets to be too much for me to handle. The pain is just too intense. I just can't stand it."

"That is why I finally had to say, 'Into Your hands I commend my Spirit.'"

"So, you just gave up? Is that what you are saying? Anyhow, I am talking about *my* grief. Can we talk about my grief? You asked **me** why I was weeping – well, I am trying to tell you, but you are just like the rest! You insert these things that are completely nonsensical and unhelpful. Why can't someone just sit with me **in** my suffering?"

"Do you mean like how you sat with me under the cross?"

My eyes open. The darkness of the night is turning into the light of the day. I can see the man in front of me much more clearly. Even more tears start flowing out of my eyes before I have a chance to think or feel. All I know is I have this awareness that my heart will implode by the sheer weight of the emotions surging through my body. My throat is so constricted that I feel as if I cannot even breathe. I realize that *my* Jesus is standing right in front of me. I want to fling myself upon his feet and kiss them.

I stammer out, "It was awful. I stayed. I stayed. I stayed through the horror. I stayed through all the tears. I stayed through the ear-piercing scream. I stayed through the blood dripping off of your side. I stayed. I stayed with the other women, and we took turns holding each other up. It was horrific. Such pain and agony – the depth of suffering I have never ever seen before. But I stayed."

"You are right. You stood under the cross. You did not turn away. You were with me in my suffering."

"So, why can so few be with me in my suffering? Why can't they stay? Why can't we just be there for one another?"

"You saw for yourself how many could stay for me. So many vowing they would never, ever leave me. And yet who else was there standing with you?"

"Oh Jesus! They love you so. We have been cooped up together. We have been crying our eyes out. None of us understood what was happening. They are feeling so guilty. They are incredibly sad. They just could not stay. They just could not stay. And I have to be honest, I was so angry with them. I wanted to scream at them at the top of my lungs. But I saw their sorrow. And, of course, because of my own grief, I just didn't have any emotional energy to scream and yell at anyone. So, we just all collapsed onto the floor and sobbed. But they love you. Oh, how they love you."

"There was so much in that '**Why**?' that I screamed." Jesus replies ever so softly.

"Yes. You were forsaken by so many. They just walked away. You poured your life into them and yet when you needed them the most they turned and ran. No wonder you thought you were forsaken by God as well. I have never heard a scream that loud. I can still hear it ringing in my ears. I might hear it for the rest of my life."

Jesus tells me, "Thank you for loving me. Thank you for standing with me. Thank you for being with me in my suffering."

Tears start cascading again down my cheeks. "Oh, dear Jesus, thank **you** for loving **me**. Thank you for standing with me. And, thank you for always being there with me in my suffering."

Write your own story #2

In this story, I use the questions that are asked of Mary Magdalene. Twice, Mary is asked "Woman, why are you weeping?" And, she is asked by Jesus "Who are you looking for?" Both questions beg each of us to answer these questions as well. How would you answer these questions for you and your circumstances? I find these questions heart-piercing. Do you? If so, how do you answer them?

> John 20:11-18: "But Mary stood weeping outside the tomb. As she wept, she bent over to look into the tomb; and she saw two angels in white, sitting where the body of Jesus had been lying, one at the head and the other at the feet. They said to her, "Woman, why are you weeping?" She said to them, "They have taken away my Lord, and I do not know where they have laid him." When she had said this, she turned around and saw Jesus standing there, but she did not know that it was Jesus. Jesus said to her, "Woman, why are you weeping? Whom are you looking for?" Supposing him to be the gardener, she said to him, "Sir, if you have carried him away, tell me where you have laid him, and I will take him away." Jesus said to her, "Mary!" She turned and said to him in Hebrew, "Rabbouni!" (which means Teacher). Jesus said to her, "Do not hold on to me, because I have not yet ascended to the Father. But go to my brothers and say to them, 'I am ascending to my Father and your Father, to my God and your God.'" Mary Magdalene went and announced to the disciples, "I have seen the Lord"; and she told them that he had said these things to her."

As I sat waiting for the correctional officers to bring over my second friend from his death row housing unit, I was drawn to this passage. I had just spent more than an hour talking with my friend who had lost his final appeal, which means now the state can set his execution date. Our conversation felt deeper and more loving than it had ever been before. We had not seen each other for more than a month because I had been ill and then the prison had gone on lockdown. So, there was an excitement to us seeing each other again. There was also a gravity to our words. In my pocket was a

81

thick stack of Kleenex just waiting to be used, but which were never pulled out.

Mary runs to the tomb while it is still dark. Her eyes surely are bleary from enormous grief. As I replay the scenes of those last few days, I see her sobs starting at the sight of Jesus carrying the cross and not stopping until her grief shuts her down. She sleeps fitfully for only few hours as she has nightmares of the horrendous scene of Jesus' death replaying in her mind. As she runs to the tomb, tears stream down her face. She has a task to do. She must embalm the body. She must take care of her Jesus. She must. She must. The darkness, however, plays tricks on her, so she swerves left and right as she is unsure of her steps.

She gets to the tomb, she doesn't see Jesus' body; instead, she sees two angels. Surely, she is making them up. Surely, they are not real. Surely, her grief and the lack of sleep have gotten the better of her. Then they ask her, "Woman, why are you weeping?" She does not, she *cannot* answer their question. She instead focuses on the task at hand and asks them where they have taken Jesus. As soon as she said this, she surely felt she had to run to find him herself. But as she turns she sees another man.

This man asks her "Woman, why are you weeping? Whom are you looking for?" She doesn't recognize him to be Jesus. It is dark. Her eyes are filled with tears. She most likely cannot even look up at his face fully because it would take too much strength, just too much effort. She sputters out that she just wants him to tell her where her Jesus is. Won't somebody, *anybody*, tell her where her Jesus is!? She is exhausted. She is spent. She is grief-stricken. She is weak. She still visualizes the horror of his execution. Can't somebody tell her? Where is Jesus in the midst of all of my weeping and wailing? **Where is he!?**

As I sit in the little room alone, I start to fast forward and think about the day in which my dear friend, who I love so dearly, will be executed. My mind shuts down. I cannot think about it. It is too much. If I start to cry, I will not stop. Surely there is an "out" button that can be pushed, and this awful dream that I seem to be in the middle of will all go away. Where is the *God of the impossible* now that I need this God the most? Where is the final, final appeal that will be heard and understood that will finally end this madness?

"Woman, why are you weeping?" What else can I do? What other options do I have? The State is planning on killing my friend, my dear, dear friend. The state, that tells its citizens that murder is a horrible and awful crime, is about ready to murder someone I deeply and profoundly love. The news media with its sensationalized headlines want to turn all offenders into scum, into monsters, into the vilest pieces of skin ever produced, in order to make it easier for their readers to hate my friend and want to see him killed. The media do not care to know the real person. The media do not care to know my friend.

"Woman, why are you weeping? Whom are you looking for?" I weep because I see a system still bent on evil. I weep because I see a system that is a killing machine. I weep because I love my friend so deeply. I weep because I want to see a bit of light in all of this darkness. When will the sun come out, Jesus? When will the darkness end? And when, exactly, are you going to show up and end all of this mess? I am looking for you, Jesus! I am looking for the resurrected Jesus who can make all things new and end this horror before it even begins. Wasn't your death enough? Do we have to keep repeating it? How **many** tears need to be shed? How many lives need to be completely destroyed? I am looking for you, Jesus! So, tell me, when are you going to show up? When?!

Write your own sermon for those on the inside

Here is a sermon that could be preached for a congregation inside or outside the walls. In this sermon, I again try to live into the feelings of not only Mary Magdalene, but Jesus' mother, Mary. I try to show how these women, who were marginalized at times, are fully embraced by Jesus.

The Tale of Two Marys

<u>John 20:11-18:</u> "But Mary stood weeping outside the tomb. As she wept, she bent over to look into the tomb; and she saw two angels in white, sitting where the body of Jesus had been lying, one at the head and the other at the feet. They said to her, "Woman, why are you weeping?" She said to them, "They have taken away my Lord, and I do not know where they have laid him." When she had said this, she turned around and saw Jesus standing there, but she did not know that it was Jesus. Jesus said to her, "Woman, why are you weeping? Whom are you looking for?" Supposing him to be the gardener, she said to him, "Sir, if you have carried him away, tell me where you have laid him, and I will take him away. " Jesus said to her, "Mary! " She turned and said to him in Hebrew, "Rabbouni! " (which means Teacher). Jesus said to her, "Do not hold on to me, because I have not yet ascended to the Father. But go to my brothers and say to them, 'I am ascending to my Father and your Father, to my God and your God. " Mary Magdalene went and announced to the disciples, "**I have seen the Lord**;" and she told them that he had said these things to her."

Prayer: While we sat in darkness, Lord Jesus Christ, you interrupted us with your life. Make us, your people, a holy interruption so that by your Spirit's power we might live as a light to the nations, even as we stumble through this world's dark night. Amen.[2]

I have often thought about the women who played such a prominent part of the life of Jesus. In John 19:26, we have Mary, the mother of Jesus, underneath the cross with her sister Mary and Mary Magdalene. And in our Gospel text this morning, Mary Magdalene is at the tomb. I want to focus this morning on our two Marys: Mary, the mother of Jesus, and Mary Magdalene. I also want to address the questions that Jesus asks, "Woman, why are you weeping?" and "Who is it you are looking for?"

Jesus' mother, Mary. Everything starts with her. She is the one who gives herself fully to God. She is the one who heard from the angel that she would become pregnant and give birth to God's only Son - that with God nothing is impossible (Luke 1:35-37) – to which she replied some of the most remarkable words in Scripture "Let it be according to your Word" (Luke 1:38).

As a very young girl, she then gave birth to Jesus. She heard the angels and all of creation rejoice at the mere sight of Jesus. She watched him grow as a teenager – as a man. She heard him say that his *real* home is at the synagogue and not with her. She knew his destiny was so far past what she could hope for or imagine. She watched him heal, deliver, and bring back to life.

The fullness in her heart and soul must have been at times too much to take in. The hallelujahs to God must have been more than her heart could sing. And then all at once the hallelujahs end. Her

---

[2] Claiborne, Shane, Wilson-Hartgrove, Jonathan, and Okoro, Enuma, *Common Prayer: A Liturgy for Ordinary Radicals*, Grand Rapids, MI, Zondervan, 2010, 209.

lament starts. Her tears flow down her cheeks faster than she could have ever thought possible.

I imagine her praying something like this: "How many tears does one body have, Lord? How many tears? You say you collect them all... but surely now even all of Heaven cannot contain them. My baby boy is being falsely accused of crimes he did not commit. He came in love and they are only spitting hatred at him. He is sinless and yet they will send him to death row to die between two criminals. Why God? Why?"

And then Mary, the mother of Jesus, had to watch minute by agonizing minute as her Son died on that cross. She must have sobbed over every drop of blood that fell to the ground. She must have screamed to Heaven as she watched the crown of thorns pierce his head that she had kissed a thousand times when he was a babe in her arms. She must have wailed as the nails were driven into those hands and feet she first examined when he was born to make sure there were 10 precious fingers and 10 exquisite toes. Each of his screams must have pierced her heart like 100,000 daggers.

I can see her being held up by other women. Her legs have lost their ability to stand. Her heart aches. Her tongue is dry. She cannot speak any more. All she can do is cry. And, she is so dehydrated that she literally runs out of tears. As Jesus' limp body is taken off of the cross, so Mary's limp body is taken home.

As Jesus' body is laid behind a boulder, so Mary's body is sequestered away for her to lament. No words are spoken. This, after all, is the time of *Shiva*. There can be a muteness to grief. Stare. That's all you can do. You give big eyes to all who come near – those eyes screaming the unspoken questions at all who see them: "What just happened? Where is my loved one? Where is my Son? Where is my Jesus?"

If I allow myself to "feel" for Mary, I feel tightness in my chest. I keep thinking that my heart literally will implode from the grief. My mind races constantly with thoughts – with remembrances – with the trauma of the events of the Cross. I dare not close my eyes or try to sleep because those trauma moments become too vivid – the crowd jeering and laughing – my friends crying and holding – the blood – oh my Lord, the blood that just kept pouring and pouring – the shouts of pain and suffering – my wailing that I could not control. No, God, no – do not let me sleep. Instead, let all of us who are grieving just hold onto each other with our very last breath.

With the little strength that she had after three days of the deepest lament this world has ever known, filled with sleepless nights, and a complete inability to move, I am imagining that Mary hears the news – she hears the news though her eyes are blurry and dazed.

"He is alive! He is alive! Why are you weeping? He is alive!"

I can feel her confusion – I can sense that her mind is trying to make sense out of what others are saying – I can feel her heart trying to be glad but feeling the enormous loss all at the same time. She stammers out the question: "Heeeee issssss alive??" The words at the incarnation are the same words that can be used for the resurrection, "With God nothing is impossible!" Can I believe it? "May it be according to **your** Word, oh God!"

And then we have Mary Magdalene. Mary Magdalene who appeared on the scene when she was healed by Jesus. The scholars disagree on which Mary was in which scene, but I have always looked at Mary Magdalene as the "sacramental" Mary. The Mary who was at Jesus' feet washing his feet with her hair – and this was before the disciples had their feet washed by Christ. Yes, Mary already knew that to follow Christ one must learn to be the servant of all.

Mary Magdalene stood at the foot of the cross with Jesus' mother through the most grueling hours a mother and a friend could ever face... she stayed while others ran. And here she is – early morning at the tomb – while it is still dark.

I am imagining she hasn't slept – that she hasn't eaten – that she has had little to drink – so her legs are trying to find their feeling without much success. But, she is determined to fulfill her task of preparing the body. This is what she should do – this is what she *must* do.

"Oh, no! No! No! No!" she screams. At a distance, she can see that the stone has been rolled away. She thinks: Stones don't just roll away. She closes her eyes – she rubs them – she is just exhausted beyond belief – this is all a mirage. This can't be real. She walks closer and closer. What is happening? The stone has rolled away.

"WHAT NOW, GOD!? What has happened to my Jesus? I cannot do this anymore. Do you hear me? Do you HEAR me? JESUS WHERE ARE YOU? My Lord, what has happened to you?"

She dare not look in – she is *afraid* to look in. She leans down and peeks in, she sees nothing; the tomb is empty. Empty. As Mary enters the tomb, I imagine the complete loss of control of her body. She must have collapsed again from the unbearable grief. Her Savior is missing. Her Savior is gone. It is then and there that the angels ask, "Woman, why are you weeping?"

In my imaginary world, I hear Mary saying in her mind, if not out loud, "*Why* am I weeping? I came here to prepare the body of my precious Savior and I find that he is gone. I am lying here in a crumpled-up ball, unable to move from my grief, and you ask me why I am weeping? What else can I do but cry? This pain is too much. I cannot go on living without Jesus, without my Savior! Don't ask me to go on without him."

But, all we hear in the Scriptures is her saying: "They have taken my Lord away, and I don't know where they have put him." I wonder how long it took her to get these words out. I wonder how many tears were shed with each word. I wonder how desperate her heart was feeling.

Then, the Gospel of John tells us:

> [14]At this, she turned around and saw Jesus standing there, but she did not realize that it was Jesus. [15]"Woman," he said, "**why are you weeping? Who is it you are looking for?**" Thinking he was the gardener, she said, 'Sir, if you have carried him away, tell me where you have put him, and I will get him.'

I sense her great grief again. I can imagine her mind wondering why everyone seems to be stuck on this question of "why I am weeping?" I can hear her screaming, "What else can I do? The person I put all of my love – and trust – and self into is dead – and now he is missing – and all you all want to do is ask me why I am a crumpled mess of grief."

And yet, Jesus asks her one more question, "Who is it you are looking for?" Notice, Mary just skips over that question and gets to the point of the matter: "Tell me where you have put him and I will get him."

You see, there is no distance that Mary won't run to in order to find her Jesus. She doesn't place blame – she just wants to find Jesus so he can be buried properly – she will run when she is out of breath – she will seek even though she can barely see through her bleary eyes – she will find him no matter what the cost.

And then, Jesus finally says, "Mary." Right at that moment, upon hearing her name, upon hearing Jesus claim her once again, she turns toward him and cries out in Aramaic, "Rabboni!" (which means Teacher).

Jesus said to her, "Do not hold on to me, because I have not yet ascended to the Father. But go to my brothers and say to them, 'I am ascending to my Father and your Father, to my God and your God.'" (John 20:17)

Even though the Scriptures don't say it, you can see Mary flinging her entire body toward Jesus in order to embrace him. But Jesus isn't just for Mary to claim. The risen Christ is for all of us.

And don't miss the fact that the first person Jesus asks to herald the Good News that he is risen is a woman. Jesus upends all social norms and gives Mary the task of telling the news to the men.

"Mary Magdalene went to the disciples and announced, **"I have seen the Lord"**; she told them that he had said these things to her. And just as breathless as she was at the tomb, she is breathless again as she exclaims with her entire being, "I have seen the Lord." (John 20:18)

Maybe a few of us came in here in the darkness of our grief and our sorrow – in the darkness of our lives – we bring with us the fresh memories of a Cross with a Savior on it – with blood just dripping down. It occurs to me that even the risen Jesus, the risen Christ, still has holes in him. The holes that remain because one's grief is just that intense.

"Put your hand in... put your hand in and you will know who I am," says Jesus to Thomas (John 20:27). As we try to be Christ to a world who needs Christ, we realize we are not perfect. As we try to be Christ we should know we ARE Christ even if we have some holes of grief still left in us.

Even in grief, there is a mixture of tears and laughter. This is one of the truths of life. Good Friday is still in our memory bank even though today is Resurrection Sunday: Lament and laughter; grief and smiles. These seeming contradictions go together. We are people who are called to remember... who are called to never forget our story. It is a story that has the greatest sorrow this world has ever known, and the story also has the greatest joy... there is the death and there is also the resurrection. Woven through the fabric of our tears and our laughter is a God who claims us with the greatest love... the purest love... the love that enfolds us and holds us.

Let us also remember: Death does not have the final say, resurrection does. Let us remember in our dying we have life that is everlasting. Let us remember that hatred does not have the final word, but love that is infinite and everlasting does.

You see this Easter morning, Jesus enters into the empty tombs of our lives and helps us to walk out knowing that Christ is there to journey with us.

And may our journey be like our two Marys – our two Marys who were vulnerable to love – who were vulnerable to God's transforming love by saying "Here I am," "Here is my life."

Our two Marys who believed with their mind, body, and souls that Jesus is the Christ – that Jesus is the RISEN Christ.

Our two Marys who became for Jesus his quintessential disciples as they stayed with him throughout his life – his death – and his resurrection.

Our two Marys who watched Jesus upend the social status, upend the notion that women were somehow less than their male counterparts by fully embracing them as co-partners in ministry.

Our two Marys who cried the cry of all of us – who cried the cry of injustice – who cried the cry of death and all of its spoils – who cried the cry of a world bent on hate – who cried the cry of all of those who are marginalized and pushed aside and who are told that somehow they are "less than."

May we be sensitive to the cries of this world – like listening to a newborn baby's cry. The cry compels an exhausted body to arise in the middle of the night – bleary eyed, completely spent – yet somehow containing enough vigor to react and move.

May our journey be like our Marys' journey.

Finally, I repeat Jesus's question: Who were you looking for this morning? Who were you hoping to see? If you came to see the risen Christ, know that he might not look like you had hoped to see him – he has holes in him after all. Maybe, Christ is the inmate who wants to sing a song he wrote for you that starts with "the God of the impossible is faithful." Maybe, Christ is the homeless person who isn't looking for handouts but just wants someone to sit a spell. Maybe, Christ is the protester who won't let the 1% set policy for the marginalized 99%.

Who were you looking for this morning? Who were you hoping to see?

Maybe Christ is sitting right next to you and maybe Christ has been sitting there all along.

Christ is risen. Christ is risen *indeed*! **Love is alive**! And the best news of all: *Love* wins!

May we journey like our Marys – vulnerable to the transforming and **living** love of Christ – this day and every day forevermore. Amen and Amen.

Write your own John 20:11-18 story

1 Samuel 16:1-13

As you read the text, listen as if you are experiencing it for the first time. Stop when something astounds you or takes you up short. Write down the feeling that you are having. Again, welcome *all* feelings, both wanted and unwanted. After reading the text, sit with it for a while as you think about each character and what each is doing and feeling at the time. This text is rich with questions and behaviors you might not expect by the various characters.

[1]The LORD said to Samuel, 'How long will you grieve over Saul? I have rejected him from being king over Israel. Fill your horn with oil and set out; I will send you to Jesse the Bethlehemite, for I have provided for myself a king among his sons.' [2]Samuel said, 'How can I go? If Saul hears of it, he will kill me.' And the LORD said, 'Take a heifer with you, and say, "I have come to sacrifice to the LORD." [3]Invite Jesse to the sacrifice, and I will show you what you shall do; and you shall anoint for me the one whom I name to you.' [4]Samuel did what the LORD commanded, and came to Bethlehem. The elders of the city came to meet him trembling, and said, 'Do you come peaceably?' [5]He said, 'Peaceably; I have come to sacrifice to the LORD; sanctify yourselves and come with me to the sacrifice.' And he sanctified Jesse and his sons and invited them to the sacrifice.

[6]When they came, he looked on Eliab and thought, 'Surely the LORD's anointed is now before the LORD.' [7]But the LORD said to Samuel, 'Do not look on his appearance or on the height of his stature, because I have rejected him; for the LORD does not see as mortals see; they look on the outward appearance, but the LORD looks on the heart.' [8]Then Jesse called Abinadab, and made him pass before Samuel. He said, 'Neither has the LORD chosen this one.' [9]Then Jesse made Shammah pass by. And he said, 'Neither has the LORD chosen this one.' [10]Jesse made seven of his sons pass before Samuel, and Samuel said to Jesse, 'The LORD has not chosen any of these.' [11]Samuel said to Jesse, 'Are all your sons here?' And he said, 'There remains yet the youngest, but he is keeping the sheep.' And Samuel said to Jesse, 'Send and bring him; for we will

not sit down until he comes here.' [12]He sent and brought him in. Now he was ruddy, and had beautiful eyes, and was handsome. The LORD said, 'Rise and anoint him; for this is the one.' [13]Then Samuel took the horn of oil, and anointed him in the presence of his brothers; and the spirit of the LORD came mightily upon David from that day forward. Samuel then set out and went to Ramah.

Phrase by phrase

Take a deep breath. Get comfortable where you are sitting. Pray that the Holy Spirit would reveal new truths to you about the story as well as about your own story. Welcome all feelings that are brought up by jotting them down in the spaces below. Again, try to hear the story as if you are hearing it for the first time.

[1]The LORD said to Samuel,

'How long will you grieve

over Saul?

I have rejected him

from being king over Israel.

Fill your horn with oil

and set out;

I will send you to Jesse the Bethlehemite,

for I have provided for myself a king

among his sons.'

²Samuel said, 'How can I go?

If Saul hears of it, he will kill me.'

And the LORD said, 'Take a heifer with you,

and say, "I have come to sacrifice to the LORD."

³Invite Jesse to the sacrifice,

and I will show you what you shall do;

and you shall anoint for me

the one whom I name to you.'

⁴Samuel did what the LORD commanded,

and came to Bethlehem.

The elders of the city came to meet him trembling,

and said, 'Do you come peaceably?'

[5]He said, 'Peaceably;

I have come to sacrifice to the LORD;

sanctify yourselves

and come with me to the sacrifice.'

 And he sanctified Jesse and his sons

and invited them to the sacrifice.

[6]When they came,

he looked on Eliab and thought,

'Surely the LORD's anointed is now before the LORD.'[*]

[7]But the LORD said to Samuel,

'Do not look on his appearance

or on the height of his stature,

because I have rejected him;

for the LORD does not see as mortals see;

they look on the outward appearance,

but the LORD looks on the heart.'

[8]Then Jesse called Abinadab,

and made him pass before Samuel.

He said, 'Neither has the LORD chosen this one.'

[9]Then Jesse made Shammah pass by.

And he said, 'Neither has the LORD chosen this one.'

[10]Jesse made seven of his sons

pass before Samuel,

and Samuel said to Jesse,

The LORD has not chosen any of these.'

[11]Samuel said to Jesse, 'Are all your sons here?'

And he said, 'There remains yet the youngest,

but he is keeping the sheep.'

And Samuel said to Jesse, 'Send and bring him;

for we will not sit down until he comes here.'

[12]He sent and brought him in.

Now he was ruddy,

and had beautiful eyes,

and was handsome.

The LORD said, 'Rise and anoint him;

for this is the one.'

[13]Then Samuel took the horn of oil,

and anointed him in the presence of his brothers;

and the spirit of the LORD came mightily upon David

from that day forward.

Samuel then set out and went to Ramah.

Questions of the text

In these questions, I have you look at each character more fully. After reviewing them, think about which character you most identify with. Think about why you identify with one character over another. What attributes of each character do you most identify with? Jot those attributes down. Again, not all questions will be relevant to you. However, some of the questions will grab you and say, "Look at me!" Write down what you are feeling when you read those questions.

¹The LORD said to Samuel, 'How long will you grieve over Saul? I have rejected him from being king over Israel. Fill your horn with oil and set out; I will send you to Jesse the Bethlehemite, for I have provided for myself a king among his sons.' ²Samuel said, 'How can I go? If Saul hears of it, he will kill me.' And the LORD said, 'Take a heifer with you, and say, "I have come to sacrifice to the LORD." ³Invite Jesse to the sacrifice, and I will show you what you shall do; and you shall anoint for me the one whom I name to you.' ⁴Samuel did what the LORD commanded, and came to Bethlehem. The elders of the city came to meet him trembling, and said, 'Do you come peaceably?' ⁵He said, 'Peaceably; I have come to sacrifice to the LORD; sanctify yourselves and come with me to the sacrifice.' And he sanctified Jesse and his sons and invited them to the sacrifice.

⁶When they came, he looked on Eliab and thought, 'Surely the LORD's anointed is now before the LORD.' ⁷But the LORD said to Samuel, 'Do not look on his appearance or on the height of his stature, because I have rejected him; for the LORD does not see as mortals see; they look on the outward appearance, but the LORD looks on the heart.' ⁸Then Jesse called Abinadab, and made him pass before Samuel. He said, 'Neither has the LORD chosen this one.' ⁹Then Jesse made Shammah pass by. And he said, 'Neither has the LORD chosen this one.' ¹⁰Jesse made seven of his sons pass before Samuel, and Samuel said to Jesse, 'The LORD has not chosen any of these.' ¹¹Samuel said to Jesse, 'Are all your sons here?' And he said, 'There remains yet the youngest, but he is keeping the sheep.' And Samuel said to Jesse, 'Send and bring him; for we will

not sit down until he comes here.' [12]He sent and brought him in. Now he was ruddy, and had beautiful eyes, and was handsome. The LORD said, 'Rise and anoint him; for this is the one.' [13]Then Samuel took the horn of oil, and anointed him in the presence of his brothers; and the spirit of the LORD came mightily upon David from that day forward. Samuel then set out and went to Ramah.

1. Imagine yourself in the narrative. Who are you? Are you Samuel? Are you one of the townspeople? Are you Jesse, the father of David? Are you one of the sons? Are you David?

   - See the whole scene in front of you. Pretend that you have a movie camera in front of you. Look through the lens viewer.
   - What are you seeing for the first time? What are you feeling?
   - What are you smelling? Are you anxious?
   - What are you hearing? Are the various scenes quiet and peaceful? Do you just hear the birds chirping in the distance? Or can you hear murmurs? Do you hear doors latching shut?
   - What are you feeling? Are you feeling God's peace? Or is there an anxiety in your belly?

2. Imagine that you are Samuel.

   - God is asking you, "How long will you grieve over...?"
     - What are you grieving over that is keeping you from going on the journey God has in front of you? Why do you feel stuck?
     - Do you feel God close to you? Do you feel that God is far away from you?
     - How do you answer God's question on "how long..."?
   - God is giving a directive to "fill your horn with oil and set out." How does that feel?

- Do you want to willingly follow the command that God gives? Or, are you saying "no" to God and listing all of the reasons why you can't go?
- What do you think is the significance of adding the oil to the horn?

- God might have rejected Saul as king, but Saul is *still* king! How do you make sense of God when God seemingly doesn't make sense?
  - God is even very specific with exactly where this new king will be found. But everyone knows that no reigning king wants to hear of a new king even if he is God ordained.
  - So how do you feel about your mission? Do you feel it is dangerous? Scary? Do you feel at peace?

- You reply to God, "How can I go?" The whole plan sounds zany. God isn't sending an army; God is sending one prophet.
  - What items are on the list of things that keep you from going on the journey that God wants you to go on? What rationalizations are you telling God? Samuel is afraid of being killed (with good reason!). What are you afraid of?
  - The call of God can be risky! How can you move forward in peace and not in fear?

- God tells you to take a heifer with you on the journey. What good would a cow do?
  - Does the heifer sound like a burden? Could it somehow be a blessing?
  - Are there extra things that you are asked to carry or that you are carrying now that seem more like a curse than a blessing?

- God tells you to say "I have come to sacrifice to the Lord." Do you think your journey will be one of sacrifice?
  - What will God give you (potentially) to sacrifice somewhere along the way?
  - Has this already happened in your life? If so, explain.
- God tells you to invite the father of one of the sons who is to be king to this sacrifice. What does this say about *community*? Is God saying that you will do it all on your own? Or, is God saying that others will be with you?
- God informs you that once the invitation for the sacrifice is given then God will tell you what to do. In your journey, do you feel you are being asked to trust and believe with each step even though you don't know what is ahead? How does that feel? Especially on top of the fact that this is a "risky adventure" that God is calling you to go on?
  - Do you feel like you are being called to jump in the deep end of the pool with no visible sign of God's arms?
  - Do you trust that God will be there for you? If you trust, where does that come from?
- God specifies your task: Anoint who God identifies. Do you feel your purpose in life is this holy?
  - Do you see that God is calling you out to anoint, to bless, to make sacred another one's life – someone that God knows by name?
  - Do you see yourself as the hands and feet of Christ?
- You do as God commands, but you are met by people who are literally quaking in their footwear

when they see you. Are you always warmly received by others when you are following God's path for you?

- How do you handle resistance?
- What do you say to those who might want to deter you?

- The community asks you, "Do you come peaceably?"
  - How do you present yourself? Are you a force to be reckoned with? Are you humble? Aggressive? Quiet?
  - Do you gauge your leadership based upon the situation?

- You let everyone know that you come peacefully. You invite everyone to the sacrifice, and you even sanctify everyone. What extra steps do you take with the community to prepare them for the mission to which you are called?
  - Is there something that you need to specifically do for them to win them over?
  - Is there something further that needs to be explained?

- Notice the townspeople were invited to a sacrifice as well as Jesse and his family.
  - Have you felt like God was asking you to sacrifice something? What is it that you might have to sacrifice?
  - God gave Samuel the cow. Has God given you something only to ask you to give it up later?

- Samuel is very sure that the anointed is in front of him when he sees Eliab, but God says, "Do not look on his appearance or on the height of his stature, because I have rejected him; for the LORD does not see as mortals see; they look on the outward appearance, but the LORD looks on the heart."

- Are you glad that God looks at one's heart, one's motives, and one's desires for God above a person's outward appearance and/or credentials?
- Or, do you wish that God would be more reasonable?

- How do you feel about the "parade of sons" going on? What is happening to your faith?
  - Has God ever sent you somewhere only to say one "no" after another "no"? Close one door after another door? What do you do? Do you let God "have it"? Do you let God "have it" after each "no"?
  - Or with all of those "no's" do you maintain a positive faith journey?
  - Or, do you enter into the "dark night of the soul"?
  - What was your faith like before and after each journey where you were getting God's "no" instead of "yes"? How deep was your relationship with God before and after the journey?
  - Have you ever had your final "yes" come in the form of a person that wasn't even in the group of possible candidates? Maybe a homeless person who is like David and hasn't been able to bathe in weeks? An incarcerated person on death row who is tending his own sheep on the row?

- You realize that Jesse hasn't told you the whole truth about his sons. How do you handle it when people around you tell you lies that hold up your progress?
    - Do you get angry?
    - Do you confront them in love?

- You refuse to sit down until the last son is brought to you. Are there times in your life when you think you need to "stand" in your truth? If so, when was it and what happened?
- Right after you are told not to look at one's appearances, you are still given a full description of the youngest son: "Now he was ruddy, and had beautiful eyes, and was handsome." Is it a blessing or a curse to judge someone by the way they look? Explain.
- God is clear, "this is the one," and so you take your oil and anoint the youngest son. It was then that the Holy Spirit came mightily upon him. Have you had an experience where someone you were ministering to was overcome by the Holy Spirit? Were you happy? Scared? Overwhelmed yourself?
- How does it feel to have your task completed? Do you feel a sense of peace? Sadness? Do you ask God right away, "What is next"? Or, do you take some time for Sabbath rest?
3. Imagine that you are the elders in the town:
    - Why are you shaking just seeing Samuel? Why are you so afraid of him?
        - Has there been a time when you were shaking just being in the presence of your pastor, priest, rabbi, or imam?
        - If so, what happened?

108

- Samuel asks you to sanctify yourself and come to the sacrifice.
    - Do you do as you are told? Or, do you hang back and see how it goes with the others in the town?
    - What is your typical course of action?
4. Imagine that you are Jesse:
    - Samuel sanctifies you. How does this feel? Are you afraid? Are you uplifted?
    - Samuel invites you and your sons to the sacrifice. However, you do not invite all of your sons. Why is that?
        - Why do you hold back on your youngest son? Does this say something about how afraid you are? Are you not trusting this very holy moment?
        - Have you ever held back something from God maybe at your baptism? Your ordination? Your catechism? Was it a part of you? Why did you hold it back?
    - Jesse is told by Samuel to go get David. Have you ever been asked to do something by your pastor, priest, rabbi, or imam that did not make sense to you? Did you do it anyhow? Or, did you say that you wouldn't do it? Explain.
5. Imagine that you are Eliab. Most likely, Samuel would have started with the eldest son. During those times, the eldest would have been the "most qualified." What does it feel like to be dismissed immediately?
    - Have you ever wanted a job and were not even given an interview even though you knew you were more qualified than others?

- How does it feel to be "rejected" by God for the task?
6. Imagine that you are David:
  - You are out tending your sheep. You might not have bathed for days on end. You have been summoned – even ordered – to come back home immediately and leave your sheep behind. How are you feeling?
    - Do you feel because you are a smelly and lowly shepherd that you aren't worthy?
    - Have you ever been called by God to leave everything you knew and loved in order to follow God? What was that like? How did that feel? Was it scary? Exciting?
  - You are brought in to the room full of all of your family members and the holy prophet of God, Samuel. You hear the words from God, "Rise and anoint him; for this is the one." What are you thinking?
    - Are you wondering "anoint him for what?!" You really are anointed without your permission (seemingly), how does that feel?
    - Have you ever blindly followed God's call in the confidence of God's care? Or, do you have to make sure of God's call first?
  - At some point, you realize that you weren't summoned earlier which means that no one in the room thought that you were actually "qualified" to do the job. How does that feel to you?
    - Have others disqualified you before even hearing your call story?
    - If they did disqualify you right away, why did they?

- The Holy Spirit comes on you in a *mighty way*.
  - Do you have an experience of being filled with the Holy Spirit in such an overwhelming way? What was that like for you?
  - Did the experience empower your ministry ahead? Was it frightening?

Write your own story #1

Here, I write a story using just the shortened question from the first verse of the chapter. Many of us grieve continuously the death of someone we love. I believe God is saying that we should not get stuck in our grief where it is like quicksand. However, I do not read this question to say "stop grieving." I am positive that God wants us to grieve and to grieve well the death of one that is so beloved, no matter how long that takes.

> 1 Samuel 16:1: "The LORD said to Samuel, 'How long will you grieve...?'"

I have been around a lot of death and dying the past 12 years. It never gets easier. Never. Each death is unique. Dying brings with it its own bits of trauma to one's soul. Each life is special. Each person is to be uniquely celebrated. Each one we loved with such great intensity is to be grieved and to be grieved well. I have sat with many people on their mourning benches – silently, wordlessly. I sat just being a loving presence in the enormity of their grief.

I often tell people that grief is like the waves of the ocean against the sand. There are times when the waves are so very calm and serene that you literally feel as if you could fall asleep by its rhythm and beat. There are other times when the waves crash in - the sheer weight of the water could pull you under and you would never be seen again.

My dear girlfriend and I were at dinner the other night when her whole body erupted in tears. I reached out my hands and held her hands. After a few moments, I simply asked her son's name, "David?" You see, her beloved son – the child so perfectly and beautifully made especially for her – had died, and the grief of his death is ever-present. "Yes, do you see that boy?" she asked. I turned around and saw a small boy who could have been David as a toddler. I simply said to her, "A loss as profound as his you never get over. Never, ever."

She then said something I will never forget, "some people say, grief comes and goes. That is not the truth. It just comes." It was as if a light went on over my brain as I said back to her, "It just comes. Oh, my! It just comes." And I thought right away of my waves on the sand without speaking of them. The waves along the shore do not stop. They do not end. They do not cease. They keep coming. They keep rolling in. The metaphor that I have been using for all of these years has been given new eyes, a new light to see more clearly the truth of it. The grief it just comes over and over and over and over again.

For some deaths, we simply will not "get over it." We need to know that. Some deaths are too traumatic for our systems, too great a loss, too much for our souls, too significant for our lives. The grief just keeps coming like the waves on the beach. Do we want those waves to end? No. But we learn somehow to swim in those waters – to befriend them – to let them wash over us – to nourish our souls in a way through their sound, their saltiness, and their warmth. But be careful, they are also treacherous at times as they can be all-consuming and overwhelming. The waters burst with force and fury to the point that they will not be denied; anyone and anything in their way is swept up and taken away.

The grief, it just comes over and over and over again. May each of us have God's grace to face those grief waters with the One who knows the number of hairs on our head, the names of each of the stars in the sky, and who has written each of our names in the palm of the Almighty's hand.

Write your own story #2

Here, I take another humorous look at the Scripture as I tell of my own call story. You should feel free to add in a good dose of humor. Scripture contains quite a bit of humor in it, and you therefore should feel equally able to add a little "tongue and cheek" to your writing.

> 1 Samuel 16:4: "Samuel did what the Lord said. When he arrived at Bethlehem, the elders of the town trembled when they met him. They asked, 'Do you come in peace?'"

Samuel has been called by God to ordain a new king. But, here's the kicker – there is already a king on the throne. And yet, God says "go" and so Samuel, with a cow in tow, heads off to find a new king. You know, the usual way you dethrone kings – with a single wild-haired prophet and a knobby kneed cow. Isn't this how it always happens, right? Forget about a large army to overthrow the reigning king! Who needs that?!?

Sometimes, our calls from God seem equally as ludicrous! "You want me to do what!? Where!? How!? Seriously, God!?" And our dear sweet Samuel questions God, "'How can I go? If Saul hears of it, he will kill me.'" Yes, overthrowing governments is cause for the death penalty. But God simply replies, "Take a heifer with you, and say, 'I have come to sacrifice to the LORD.' Invite Jesse to the sacrifice, and I will show you what to do. You shall anoint for me the one who I name to you." Oh, okay, God; that makes perfect sense!

So, it is no surprise that he is greeted with great skepticism. The townspeople are wondering what in the world he is up to. "What is this prophet doing now? Why is he here in our town? Why is he bothering to be with us? Can't he find a better place to do ministry? And does he come in peace or is there something sinister going on?" In other words, we might say "yes!" to the zany and crazy call that God has on our life, but those around us might end up quaking in their boots.

114

I will never forget telling my parents that I had quit my corporate vice president job to follow the call God had on my life. My sweet father, with tears running down his cheeks, asked, "But, does it pay?" He didn't have to worry about me too much while I was bringing in the big bucks, but now… well now, for one of the few times in his life he was visibly shaking at the prospect of me being unemployed or unpaid. The whole *call* thing had him trembling.

Similarly, when I knew God had called me to death row, several people who were around me wanted God to get me out of the mess God had gotten me into. They were shivering and shaking at the whole notion of me spending time – even one minute of time - with guys who had committed murder. Surely, I would not be safe. Surely, God had *not* called me. Surely nothing good was going to come of such an insane call; especially, not peace!

Yet, God sent me with my driver's license and Bible in hand to sit with the guys on the row and just be present for them. I would not be dissuaded from the destination God had set for me. I had to follow my call. You see, God's call is never, ever to death. God's call is always about life – abundant life. God's call is to God's shalom – God's peace.

And I found, like Samuel, many a David behind those walls – men who had a heart for God – men who were full of the Spirit of God. And also, those who were not thought to be worthy of being in the room of people who could possibly be God's chosen ones and yet were! I had already done enough prison ministry that I knew that they would teach me more about Jesus than anyone else, and I have yet to be proven wrong. Week after week, they are Christ to me. They open up Scripture in ways that I simply cannot imagine – I just do not have their eyes – I do not live in their social location.

Some say that I go to death row. Hmmm. That might be what the warden calls it. That might be what the prison system calls it. But for me, it is life row. It is life row where laughter ensues, gospel songs are sung, Scripture is illuminated, and God's amazing love

115

reigns. How could it be otherwise? Christ is there. Ah, let me rephrase, the risen Christ is there.

Write your own sermon for those on the inside

In this sermon, I will illumine (hopefully!) the Scripture by taking it verse by verse. When you have a narrative story like this, I find it easier to preach this way as it involves everyone within your congregation in the story. I wrote this sermon for my friends on the inside. You will see how I use their social location within it.

1 Samuel 16:1-13: [1]"The LORD said to Samuel, 'How long will you grieve over Saul? I have rejected him from being king over Israel. Fill your horn with oil and set out; I will send you to Jesse the Bethlehemite, for I have provided for myself a king among his sons.' [2]Samuel said, 'How can I go? If Saul hears of it, he will kill me.' And the LORD said, 'Take a heifer with you, and say, "I have come to sacrifice to the LORD." [3]Invite Jesse to the sacrifice, and I will show you what you shall do; and you shall anoint for me the one whom I name to you.' [4]Samuel did what the LORD commanded, and came to Bethlehem. The elders of the city came to meet him trembling, and said, 'Do you come peaceably?' [5]He said, 'Peaceably;

I have come to sacrifice to the LORD; sanctify yourselves and come with me to the sacrifice.' And he sanctified Jesse and his sons and invited them to the sacrifice.

[6]When they came, he looked on Eliab and thought, 'Surely the LORD's anointed is now before the LORD.' [7]But the LORD said to Samuel, 'Do not look on his appearance or on the height of his stature, because I have rejected him; for the LORD does not see as mortals see; they look on the outward appearance, but the LORD looks on the heart.' [8]Then Jesse called Abinadab, and made him pass before Samuel. He said, 'Neither has the LORD chosen this one.' [9]Then Jesse made Shammah pass by. And he said, 'Neither has the LORD chosen this one.' [10]Jesse made seven of his sons pass before Samuel, and Samuel said to Jesse, 'The LORD has not chosen any of these.' [11]Samuel said to Jesse, 'Are all your sons here?' And he said, 'There remains yet the youngest, but he is keeping the sheep.' And Samuel said to Jesse, 'Send and bring him; for we will not sit down until he comes here.' [12]He sent and brought him in. Now he was ruddy, and had beautiful eyes, and was handsome. The

LORD said, 'Rise and anoint him; for this is the one.' [13]Then Samuel took the horn of oil, and anointed him in the presence of his brothers; and the spirit of the LORD came mightily upon David from that day forward. Samuel then set out and went to Ramah."

The year was 2008 and I was sitting in a classroom at Duke Divinity where I was almost finished with our Old Testament final examination. Our professor, Dr. Chapman, asked that we exegete or interpret this 1 Samuel 16 passage. I remember the day vividly. I had not slept the night before – well I tried – but I kept tossing and turning. And not because of the Old Testament final, but for the "real" test later that evening. You see, I was facing the elders at the church who were going to ask me any question they wanted in order to see if I was ready to be ordained. I kept thinking about ALLLLL the questions that they could possibly ask:

- How do you explain to the parents of a child why God allowed their newborn to die?
- How does someone actually become "saved"?
- Can you explain the "atonement" to us?
- Where does it say in the Bible..." Oh, fill in the blank for this one!

Of course, with every answer I kept thinking, "I should remember that." "Please remember that!" All of these questions and answers only led me to a higher and higher level of anxiety so that I kept asking myself the same question I have been asking for at least seven years now: "Who am I that you are mindful of me?" "Who am I, Lord?" And so, with these questions and answers literally ringing in my ears, I stared at the Old Testament exam and this passage in 1 Samuel 16. I read the passage. I read it again. I then read it again. And then inwardly I screamed, "PLEASE, HOLY SPIRIT, show me what I need to know because I need to get to my **real** final." And then I read this again. "OH, MY" I exclaimed, "This is about ordination!"

Let's look at the Scripture:

¹The **LORD** said to Samuel, 'How long will you grieve over Saul? I have rejected him from being king over Israel. Fill your horn with oil and set out; I will send you to Jesse the Bethlehemite, for I have provided for myself a king among his sons.'

How long? How long will you grieve? These all-too-familiar words of the psalmist are now God's words. God is wondering how long Samuel will remain stuck in his present situation.

I can see Samuel sitting almost catatonic with worry and fret; he sits and moans and groans. The LORD will have none of this self-pity. God has work to be done and Samuel has to help out. God tells him that the past is past and a new day has dawned. God is saying that all of this grief you feel about Saul was *yesterday* – this is today. Samuel, you had better get ready, get prepared, because I, the Lord your God, have a new king in my sights. So, the directive is given: "Fill your horn with oil and set out."

Most of us know that question that God asks: How long? How long? How long will you allow the worries of your past to hold you back from the future I have for you? How long will you head in another direction? How long will you sit in the dark, dank, nasty smelling mouth of the fish? How long? Get up, get prepared, and set out! There have been many moments in my life when I have heard God's voice clearly to get up and to set out. Many of the days when I would go to the fifth floor of the Federal Medical Center, I would feel this way. I would think I can just sit back and drink an extra cup of coffee, but God said, "Hurry it up! I need for you to meet someone."

This happened in dramatic fashion one week. I felt like God had someone significant for me to meet, yet as I walked through the halls, nothing *dramatic* had happened. It was time for "count" and I was told I needed to get off of the hall. Yet, the Holy Spirit said, "You are not leaving yet." You might know how these arguments go; you try to rationalize with the Holy Spirit that there are *human rules* that must be followed. Yet, the Holy Spirit said back up and go into the cell. I know that I rolled my eyes and went back.

For an hour, I worshiped the Lord with a man who had to lie perfectly still day after day on his back. He became my angel of grace and mercy on the hall. When the death on the floor got to be too much, he was my reminder of resurrection. And for him, when I showed up, I was his angel to remind him that God did indeed love him. God's "set out" made a difference for us both.

Notice that Samuel does not set out with nothing in his hands. Samuel has *oil* for anointing. The journey is not about Samuel. The journey is about blessing others. Do you hear that? The journey is to bless others and affirm the giftedness of others. What is Samuel's reply?

> [2]Samuel said, 'How can I go? If Saul hears of it, he will kill me.' And the LORD said, 'Take a heifer with you, and say, "I have come to sacrifice to the LORD."

How can I go? We might laugh at this question and yet, how many of us in our call asked this same question, "How can I go?"

- How can I go? Have you counted the number of gray hairs on my head lately?
- How can I go? Have you not noticed Lord that there are bars and barbed wire all around me?
- How can I go? Have you not seen that my friends, family, and church members are still upset with me?
- How can I go? Have you not read my rap sheet?
- ***How can I go?***

Beneath this is the question I have asked the Lord at least 500 times: "Who am I?" "Who am I to go there?" "Who am I to be called to this task?" We are told here in Scripture that Samuel is afraid that Saul will kill him. Saul still is king, after all. Anointing a new king makes absolutely no sense to Samuel. The whole mandate is illogical; it is dangerous. But the Lord's words, which he gave to

Samuel **before** the journey, are right for all of us to say even to this day: "I have come to sacrifice to the Lord." This is a sacrificial journey – it is a daily laying down of our own lives as a sacrifice to the Lord. Notice, too, that the Lord tells Samuel to take a heifer with him.

I do not know how you all feel, but there are many days when I feel like I am drrrraggggginn' a big old cow around with me.

This cow might be one of our own making; you know, having those things around us that make us feel better for the journey. Well, at least I have the right credentials. Well, at least I am a part of the right church. And at other times, these cows are our inward feelings: pride, ego, self-satisfaction. I suspect in this room we have a couple of cows that each of us has dragged here.

We read further:

> "... [3]Invite Jesse to the sacrifice, and I will show you what you shall do; and you shall anoint for me the one whom I name to you." [4]Samuel did what the LORD commanded, and came to Bethlehem. The elders of the city came to meet him trembling, and said, "Do you come peaceably?" [5]He said, "Peaceably; I have come to sacrifice to the LORD; sanctify yourselves and come with me to the sacrifice." And he sanctified Jesse and his sons and invited them to the sacrifice.

Notice that Samuel is not met with open arms. This man of God is met by a gaggle of elders from the city and they are all trembling or, as the Hebrew translation would imply "they are quaking in their boots."

If this were a movie, I can see all of the women and children running for their homes and boarding up their windows while sending their shaking and trembling husbands out to see what Samuel is up to. This can't be good, can it? But Samuel promises that he is bringing God's *shalom* to them. It is here that Samuel uses the cow as the sacrifice for not just Jesse's family, but for the whole community. Samuel also sanctifies the community and Jesse and his sons.

This dramatic build-up in the narrative at this point let's all of us know that this is a holy moment – a sacrificial and sanctified moment that we are about ready to witness. Certainly, the next point in the story will reveal to us who is the anointed one:

> [6]When they came, he looked on Eliab and thought, "Surely the Lord's anointed is now before the Lord."

Surely, this is the one. Looks like someone who is called, smells like someone who is called, has the proper family status of one who is called, has been sanctified and purified like someone who is called. Yep, I know them when I see them; this one is called! And yet, what does the Lord whisper into Samuel's ear?

> [7]But the LORD said to Samuel, "Do not look on his appearance or on the height of his stature, because I have rejected him; for the LORD does not see as mortals see; they look on the outward appearance, but the LORD looks on the heart."

The heart? What does the heart have to do with it?

Lord, you do not understand. This one standing in front of you has been to all the right schools – he went to Harvard and then to Duke Divinity. He has the right degrees – not only a Masters of Divinity, but also a Masters of Theology **and** a Doctorate of Ministry. He has been a youth leader after all for more than five long years. He is qualified. He should be chosen. Nice that you look on the heart, but **really**, no one in our society does that. God, be **logical**!

Next, we witness a dramatic beauty pageant-like twist to the story. The "right candidates" are paraded in front of Samuel only to get one "no" after another "no":

> [8]Then Jesse called Abinadab, and made him pass before Samuel. He said, "Neither has the LORD chosen this one." [9]Then Jesse made Shammah pass by. And he said, "Neither has the LORD chosen this

one." [10]Jesse made seven of his sons pass before Samuel, and Samuel said to Jesse, "The LORD has not chosen any of these."

Our criteria of who could possibly be on the short list for God's chosen one are eliminated one by one. It doesn't seem like God even cares to read the resumes that they brought along. The answer from God is a clear and swift, "Nope not the one." So, where is the chosen one?

[11]Samuel said to Jesse, "Are all your sons here?" And he said, "There remains yet the youngest, but he is keeping the sheep." And Samuel said to Jesse, "Send and bring him; for we will not sit down until he comes here."

Hear this and hear this clearly: The chosen one is not even in the room of seemingly qualified candidates.

The chosen one is some distance away, in a pasture tending the sheep.

The chosen one has not been sanctified like all the rest. No. He has been working up a sweat taking care of the sheep in the fields.

The chosen one spends all of his time with sheep. What in the world does he know about being the king of a country?

God certainly does not call young, smelly, unsanctified, inexperienced sheep herders! We know that!

Notice that Samuel says, "We will not sit down until he comes here." I don't know if there are times in your life where you just stood until the answer to prayer happened, but there will be times in your life where you need to just stand. You need to be an immovable object until the answer comes from God. You need to stand in place and see your breakthrough happen. There are times when you need to say with Samuel, "Welllllll I am not going to sit down until the answer comes." This is faith. This is what standing on the word of God means.

And then we hear that the one not in the room is the one:

¹²He sent and brought him in. Now he was ruddy, and had beautiful eyes, and was handsome. The LORD said, 'Rise and anoint him; for this is the one.'

Notice with me: The very last one in line is the first. The smelly shepherd wafts a beautiful fragrance to the Lord. The shepherd boy would be **the** one to shepherd a nation for God. The one, who by all "appearances" is not the one, **is** the chosen one.

In other words, this one who no one even thought worthy of being in the same room with others is now going to be anointed – is now going to be ordained:

¹³Then Samuel took the horn of oil, and anointed him in the presence of his brothers; and the spirit of the LORD came mightily upon David from that day forward. Samuel then set out and went to Ramah.

This anointed one is now full of the Spirit to go forth and serve the Lord. The presence of God would be with him from that day forward. The presence of God was not going to be a faint whisper either. The Spirit came upon David in a mighty way to mark the moment, to seal his fate, and to let David now know in no uncertain terms, "You are who I have called." All God cared about is whether this anointed one had a heart for serving God. This was **the** criterion.

Maybe you are asking of the Lord, "Who am I? Who am I that you are mindful of me?" But maybe God is asking you a question in return, "HOOOOOWWWWW LONGG?" How long will you keep doing your own thing? How long before you answer my call?

I need you to get up, get going, and get out! I have people for you to go and see and touch – to anoint them with my oil of blessing – to encourage them along their call. Maybe you are asking, "How can I go?"

"How can I go? You might not have noticed God, but I am behind these bars. God, you surely do not call *inmates*. We all know that;

don't be ridiculous, God!" But maybe God is saying to you, "I chose you." Maybe God is calling you to just "be a voice of love and compassion" to just one of the guys you meet on the yard. Maybe God is calling you to be in covenant with another brother in your pod where you pray for each other and read Scripture together. Maybe God is calling you to be more available to your children by writing them notes of love and encouragement. Maybe God is calling you to be a better husband to your wife, so you spend more time with Christians brothers who can give you great advice, so then you can pass on what you learned to another brother who is struggling in his marriage.

The road will be one of sacrifice, but it will be a sacrifice of love. A love beyond compare – because it has been a free-flowing love of Christ through you to others. Let me make sure you hear this: It is during these times that you see God most clearly and feel the mighty presence of the Holy Spirit. This road God puts in front of us will not be easy. The call on all of our lives is illogical, a bit dangerous, and definitely sacrificial; however, it is the greatest life we could ever imagine.

Let us be clear, we do this not for ourselves or for **our** glory, but rather to bless and be a blessing to others for God's glory – and God's glory alone.

Notice, too, it is a call to those who are not even in the room.

You will be called to those who everyone else has discounted – to say to them, "Yes, you **are** chosen - whether you feel like you have the right qualifications or not. God looks at your heart and that is what is important to God."

We might wonder how in the world we can do all that the Lord has set before us, but we can rest assured that God is with us in a **mighty** way through God's Holy Spirit. ALL we will need for our journey is a **heart for God**... maybe just the **heart of Christ**.

May it be so. May it be so. Amen and amen.

Write your own 1 Samuel 16:1-13 story

Writing your own story with sacred texts

Now that you have learned how to live into the narrative of God in the Bible, you can choose to use just one line from the Bible or another sacred text. And what do I mean by *sacred text*? A sacred text is anything you read and, as you read it, you hold it to your heart (literally or figuratively) because it deeply touches your soul. It is *sacred* to you. It is not a "head" thing' it is a "heart-piercing" thing.

Sacred texts can be found in the Bible, the Quran, or a devotional. A saying from a mystic, a quotation from various theologians, or any other writing that you deem sacred to your own life can be your sacred text. In other words, there is no right or wrong sacred text – it is sacred because your heart says so.

Some short scriptures that I personally have found both sacred and heart-piercing are:

"Those who sit in darkness have seen a great light."	Matthew 4:16
"For unto us a son is born; unto us a son is given."	Isaiah 9:8
"For with God nothing shall be impossible."	Luke 1:37
"The spirit lifted me up and took me away and I went in bitterness in the heat of my spirit, the hand of the Lord being strong upon me; and I came to the exiles at Telabib, who dwelt by the river Chebar. And I sat there overwhelmed among them seven days."	Ezekiel 3:14-15
"When John heard in prison what the Messiah	Matthew 11:2-5

was doing, he sent word by his disciples and said
to him, "Are you the one who is to come, or are
we to wait for another?" Jesus answered them,
"Go and tell John what you hear and see: the
blind receive their sight, the lame walk, the lepers
are cleansed, the deaf hear, the dead are raised,
and the poor have good news brought to them.""

"Speak, for your servant is listening."	1 Samuel 3:10
"Remember the long way that the Lord your God has led you..."	Deuteronomy 8:2
"Come to me, all you who are weary and burdened, and I will give you rest. Take my yoke upon you and learn from me, for I am gentle and humble in heart, and you will find rest for your souls. For my yoke is easy and my burden is light."	Matthew 11:28-30

Matthew 4:16

This is an example of fully thinking through the ramifications of one small piece of Scripture. To be honest, I keep adding to this story as I realize the depth that you can go into the darkness. I also realize how *illuminating* the light can be if you sit with God in the darkness.

Darkness and Light

Matthew 4:16: "Those who sit in darkness have seen a great light."

"Oh, please come out of the darkness into the light. Yes, that is better. Now…. let me look at you. You have grown a bit, haven't you? Yes, I can see it now. Isn't this better?" Wait, wait. Where are you going?"

"Oh, come out of the darkness into the light!" scream many family members and friends. But this is where I am – I am in the darkness. It surrounds me. It enfolds me. It engulfs me. I think of how many parts of my body are not just in the darkness, but in the dark recesses of my body. You know all of those hidden places that make it difficult for even the best of surgeons to get to. I have thought so much over the past many months that the places that hurt me the most are there – those darkest of recesses – those hidden-away places. My spleen, my pancreas, my liver – they are all in the dark. Not until lately did I think about my heart being there, too. I think this is rather odd that I did not think of it first. I mean, I am known for my caring heart – my *loving heart* – how I give to others out of the love of my heart. But because it is literally not giving me pain, I never realized how hidden it is, too. Yet, the pain in my heart – emotional as it might be – is still a very deep and a very real pain. I need it to see the light of day, too – to be healed – to be well – to be whole. "Oh, come out of the darkness into the light!"

"Oh. come out of the darkness into the light!" In the darkness of my womb, I co-created with God in order to give birth to Luke.[3] Two strange little organisms came together and then started bursting with joy by doubling and re-doubling and then doubling again. Each little cell knowing exactly what it needed to go and do and be – "Yes, I will be the little finger!" "Well, I am off to make the nose." "Hahaha, I get to be the big toe!" "Yes, but look at me over here, I get to be the rear." Soon enough, Luke had two very large feet that could do the cha-cha in my belly at night in order to give his father and me endless amounts of laughter. And then into the light he came. We counted his toes. We counted his fingers. And yes, I had to scream at the top of my lungs at what made him uniquely male. "Oh, come out of the darkness into the light!"

"Oh, come out of the darkness into the light!" I get cranky soon after my birthday, which is in mid-September. You see, I realize that the days are getting shorter. The summer days filled with light shorten little bit by little bit. And it creeps up on you – really, it does. You look around and realize that the sun is setting a lot earlier than you are comfortable with. Then, that dreaded day called the *shortest day* looms on the horizon. I have never liked that day. It always feels too dark – just way too dark. We try to mark days like that with rites and rituals – things that name our sadness and our grief – things that allow us to mourn the darkness in our own lives. We do so by lighting candles for our loved ones who have died during the year. We say, "I remember and, no, I won't forget." "Oh, come out of the darkness into the light!" Let's not stay in the darkness too long – especially the darkness of our grief – that could be dangerous you know. Plus, most of us who sit in the light only

---

[3] Jobe, Sarah., *Creating with God: The Holy Confusing Blessedness of Pregnancy*, Brewster, MA, Paraclete Press, 2011. In chapter 1 Rev. Jobe discusses her thoughts on "co-creating with God."

deal in *happy* so *sad* doesn't work well for us. "Oh, come out of the darkness into the light!" Not yet. What? Not yet?! The darkness of my grief needs tending to. I might see you when the Spring comes. Right now, I need to mourn my child – my beautiful, beautiful child. I don't think a week is enough – do you? Or a month – is it enough? Or two months – it feels too short. He was my beloved – truly beloved. Does grief have an end? Should grief end for one so precious? For one whom I loved with my entire being? Should grief reallllly end? "Oh, come out of the darkness into the light!"? Do I dare? Do I want to? Maybe I will just sit in the darkness for a while. I might be here for a year or two. Hmmmm. I might be here the rest of my life as my beautiful child was just that magnificent to my heart. Please understand. Will you understand?

"Oh, come out of the darkness into the light!" I have friends who struggle with mental illness. There is a "get better immediately" pill for such things, right?" "Uh, well, errrrrr, no...." I have learned to just sit in the darkness with them. I affirm that they are people of worth even when they are *in the darkness*. I sit some more. I let that suffocating silence surround me even though at times I think I can hardly breathe. And then, I sit some more. I ask them: "What are you feeling?" I affirm their feelings. Feelings, oh by the way, are always real. Like chocolate, or bunny rabbits, or stars in the sky – they are always real. So, I affirm them and say how hard it all must be. And I know it to be the truth anyhow – because as I sit, in the darkness, I can feel what they feel, I can sense what they sense – somewhat – a little bit – a glimpse or two. So, I say with assurance that it is hard as I squirm in my seat. And I wait. As I wait for their light – not my light - to break through. It will. You will see. Then – and only then – can we both walk – hand in hand – out into the light. But I have to wait. "Oh, come out of the darkness into the light!"? We will wait in the darkness until your time comes.

"Oh, come out of the darkness into the light!" Years ago, Rabbi Sager asked us to read Genesis 1 as if we had never, ever heard it before. He asked us to hear it like that little child in front of the grandparent just waiting for them to turn the page and hear what happens next. Hear it for the first time?! Hmmm – the first time. It didn't take me long at all to me to say, "Wwaaiiitt a minute! What's this?" The light wasn't created until the first day (ah, yes, you know, the third verse). What came first was the darkness, the formless void... tthhaatt is where God was?!? God was in the dark?! What was God doing in the dark?! Maybe God was in the dark to remind us when we fall into the formless pits of our lives and we think that we cannot find God there – well, God **is** there – God started there – God will stay there with you, in the dark, in the void, in the dank darkness knowing one day that light will come – one day – you know, the first day. "Oh, come out of the darkness into the light!" Ah, dear God, thank you that I am quite content to sit in the darkness with you before you even began creating.

"Oh, come out of the darkness into the light!" I also love in the Genesis passage that God gave space for both light *and* dark. God did not judge that one was "bad" and one was "good." As God was creating and bedazzling the earth with iridescent blue fish, an orange orangutan, a chameleon that changes color depending upon its surroundings, and of course drooling St. Bernards, God said it **all** was good. The light; good. The dark; good. We need the dark to see the stars after all. How could we lie on our backs and look up and see the splendor of the eclipses of the moons if it wasn't dark outside? It all is good. In fact, we are now learning that dark energy and dark matter actually make up 95% of our universe. Astounding, isn't it? And yet, there still is a balance to life: light – dark – dark – light. Do – rest – rest – do. "Oh, come out of the darkness into the light!?" "Oh, come out of the light into the darkness!?"

"Oh, come out of the darkness into the light!" Every night as I lay my head down on the pillow I do a review of the day. Who did I see? What did I do? What did I say? What would I have done differently? Who is still on my heart? Who am I still grieving for? Who do I still need to pray for? I share all of these things with Jesus. I take what is on my heart and place it on Jesus' heart. I learned this from praying with a Franciscan Friar the "Novena of Confidence to the Sacred Heart." One line goes like this: "Sacred Heart of Jesus, I have asked You for many favors, but I earnestly implore this one. Take it, place it in Your Open Heart." When I said that line the first time as I sat next to this beloved Friar, I sobbed. I literally could not go on with the rest of the prayer for some time. We just sat in silence – holding hands – staring at each other – you know the stare – "I know, it touches you in a very deep place, doesn't it?" "Why yes, it does." – but those words aren't spoken, they are just known. Some nights, the darkness is unbearably dark – it invades every cell of my body and creeps into my blood stream to stop my body's functioning. My cry of lament "How long, oh Lord?" or just that simple but ear-piercing "Why?!" might be uttered. So many tears fall that my pillow is soaked. Somewhere in the night, I fall off to sleep. God sitting there beside me – crying, too. The first rays of light of the new day awaken me. My bleary eyes try to adjust – try to see – try to figure out – ahhh, this is a new day. Jesus carried all of my prayers, cares, and woes on his heart all night long. "Oh, come out of the darkness into the light!"

"Oh, come out of the darkness into the light!" Over the many years of my own pain and suffering and also spending those same years sitting next to those who suffer greatly, I have realized this plea to come out of the darkness is a human one. God never says, "Time's up. Get a move on." God is quite comfortable in both darkness and light and will stay with us wherever we are for however long we are there. God will sit with us. Cry with us. Moan with us. Bellow with us. Lament with us. All right there in the darkness. In the dank, deep, darkness. "Oh, here you are in the darkness. Can I sit a spell with you?" The Greek here for "sit" in our Gospel text means "to have a fixed abode – to dwell." Put your jammies on. Get your slippers out. "Those who sit in the darkness have seen a great light."

133

Isaiah 9:6

This is a sad and very personal story of the grief of losing my grandson and of my son and his girlfriend losing their beloved son. There are times when you can upend Scripture in order to give your reader something they were not anticipating. Writing, for me, is a wonderful way for me to get my grief out. Living into a biblical story really helps me in that regard. I wrote this piece one Christmas day.

Isaiah 9:6: "For unto us a son is born; unto us a son is given."

As a hospice volunteer, chaplain, and even pastor, I have seen my share of death over the last twelve years. I have sat next to so many as they have taken their last breath and have departed this world into the next. I have cried many tears with those who are dying, with their family members, and with their friends. Oddly enough, I have also laughed so hard from my belly with those same people that tears of joy sprang up in equal abundance over story after story of a life well lived.

But nothing prepared me many years ago for the day when I sat with my son and his girlfriend as the medical staff induced her labor so she could give birth to her dead son – my dead grandson. I can still envision my son, so full of compassion, sitting wordlessly, with tears in his eyes just holding his girlfriend as tightly as he could as she shook with grief. We waited for what seemed to be hours in the "prep" area of the hospital. This is not Advent-waiting. This is a kind of torture that no one should go through. We just stared at one another knowing that the depth of each other's pain was unspeakable. If we felt like we could have, we all would have probably been screaming and moaning and shaking our fists toward Heaven asking the question with the loudest of voices "**Why**??!!" But, we were too civilized. So, we just held our pain and grief in our chests and in our hearts until it felt like they would literally burst at the sheer weight of it.

Today is Christmas when we celebrate the Christmas story of a beautiful baby boy being born into this world. A boy who we would learn **is** God; Emmanuel, "God with us." This baby boy was born to an unwed mother, found by shepherds, and born in a manger. I am reminded that my grandson's story was not written – it was never told – because it seemingly ended before it could begin. But that isn't totally the truth.

My grandson would have been Lawrence Doyle Willis, IV. His mother, Cookie, doted on him, talked to him, and loved on him. She was thrilled to be a new mother again and so she was always rubbing her belly or lying still so she could see every last little movement. My son, Luke, was over the moon when he found out he was going to have a baby boy. He could not stop talking about this plan and that plan for their future together. He was ready to be a father and the best there ever was. He too loved on his son as much as he could while he was still in the womb.

And well me. I was fretting over whether I should be called "Nana," "Grandma," or "Grammy." I finally had decided on "Grammy." I pulled out all of Luke's baby books and realized most of them were too chewed on to give to a baby, so I went out and bought new baby books. I also bought new baby clothes from St. Maarten while I was there in hopes that Grammy and grandson would spend many vacation days there together.

So, my dear grandson was dearly loved right until the last minute he passed into the arms of Jesus. His story was a very short story. But barely a day goes by when I don't think about him (and his parents) and wish that he was with us. I especially think about him today. I just know he would have filled the room with smiles and most importantly, laughter. Love and hugs would have abounded as we giggled together and most likely ran around the room after one another. I will forever miss his presence in our lives and love him until I see his beautiful face in Heaven.

Luke 1:37

This is one of my all-time favorite stories. If there ever were a *resurrection story*, this is it. I prayed on a Friday, and the answer came on a Sunday! Only God could have orchestrated such an event. At times, we wonder where God has gone off to. Well, I hope this story helps you realize that God truly is the God of the impossible.

The God of the impossible

Luke 1:37: "For with God nothing shall be impossible."

Years ago, I was the Pastor of a small and loving congregation in Durham, North Carolina. After being there for about six months, I was told that my "dream job" finally was a reality. I screamed with glee at first and then within the same breath I said, "No, I can't take it. I can't leave my church. I love them too much. I have just been with them for six months. It is too soon to leave them." I was conflicted about the new job; I knew I needed to pray and pray I did. I went on retreat after retreat for three months and cried out to God to speak clearly. God kept speaking, but I didn't want to hear what God was saying.

Finally, I was sitting in the parking lot of my church and was staring at the sanctuary with tears streaming down my face. I started screaming at the top of my lungs a prayer to God in the most sarcastic tone you could imagine: "Okay God of the impossible, if you want me to leave so badly, then I want that sanctuary that is literally about ready to implode to be completely restored before I go. Okay God of the impossible, if you want me to leave then I want you to find a pastor **off cycle** – how about that? Huh? That never happens! Okay, God of the impossible, I want this church not to die, but to live and to continue on as a loving congregation." And on and on I went with my demands. Screaming and shouting to this "God of the impossible."

I screamed and prayed on Friday. On Sunday, I went to the prison to preach. It was my custom back then to preach once a month at the Bureau of Prisons at their complex called the Camp. I had barely put my little toe in the door when one of the guys said "Pastor Cari, Pastor Cari, Mr. Smith has a song from God for you." "Oh wow! Thanks!" I take two more steps and I hear again, "Pastor Cari, Pastor Cari, Mr. Smith has a song from God for you." "Yes, I heard." I walk into the courtyard. "Pastor Cari, Pastor Cari, Mr. Smith has a song from God for you." "Yes, I have been told." I walk a few feet further. "Pastor Cari, Pastor Cari, Mr. Smith has a song from God for you." I am laughing loudly at this point. "Yes, I know." I walk into the chapel. "Pastor Cari, Pastor Cari, Mr. Smith has a song from God for you." "Ha, ha, ha! Yes, I know! But someone is going to have to introduce me to Mr. Smith!"

I was then taken over to this elderly Hispanic man who is shaking from the top of his head to the bottoms of his feet. I said to him "Ever since I stepped into the building, I have heard that you have a song from God for me." "Si, si, yes, yes, Pastor Cari." "Oh, how wonderful! I can hardly wait to hear you sing it." "I don't think that I can. I am too nervous. It is too much." "You will be fine. It will be perfect no matter how you sing it. It will. The Holy Spirit will be with you. I promise you, it will be perfect no matter what." "No, no, Pastor Cari, I don't think so." "It will be. I know so. If God gave you a song, it will be perfect."

I see that he is holding a folded sheet of paper in his hands; the paper is shaking so badly that it makes a rustling noise. I ask, "Are those the lyrics there in your hands?" "Si, si, yes, yes, Pastor Cari." "Could I read them? I would love to know what God is trying to say to me." "Si, si."

I take the paper in my hands as if it is gold. I gingerly open the paper as I lean down next to him. I read aloud the first four lines that are all the same "The God of the impossible is faithful. The God of the impossible is faithful. The God of the impossible is faithful.

The God of the impossible is faithful." I don't know at which line I started to cry, but when I did, I started sobbing. I looked at my friend and said "Yes, this **is** a song from God for me. Thank you so very much. God will be with you as you sing this, please know that. Thank you again so very much."

And sure enough, the God of the impossible was faithful. Every single thing that I prayed for came true. In fact, the next day our fellowship hall flooded in epic proportions so we received a very large check from the insurance company that paid off a very good chunk of the restoration work for our sanctuary. A pastor was found off-cycle so that I could start my new position. And the loving congregation has continued to love on everyone that walks through the doors of the church. The God of the impossible **is** faithful! The God of the impossible **is** faithful!

Ezekiel 3:14-15

As you start to "live into the narrative" of Scripture, you find yourself stopping yourself whenever something makes your heart skip a beat. All of the sudden as you start to slow down and read each word with great intentionality, words pop off the page as never before. This is what happened right before I wrote this next piece. As you will see, it was "unwelcomed" popping. As I was reading Scripture I didn't want to read and yet I was learning to accept all of these unwanted thoughts and feelings as "gifts of grace" or as "gifts of love" from God. Therefore, I allowed myself to welcome this bit of Scripture and hear what it had to say to me even if it meant some very sobby tears.

My Overwhelmed Heart

> Ezekiel 3:14-15: "The spirit lifted me up and took me away and I went in bitterness in the heat of my spirit, the hand of the Lord being strong upon me; and I came to the exiles at Telabib, who dwelt by the river Chebar. And I sat there overwhelmed among them seven days."

Back in 2006, I walked into the halls of the prison with bitterness in my heart only to hear the clanging and banging of the iron doors. I kept telling myself, "Had I known this is where God would call me, I would have just stayed in my corporate job and written even bigger checks to non-profits that needed my money." The walls were gray. The floors were gray. The bars were gray. Yes, even the people looked gray to me. What was I doing here?!?!

And then, because God likes to laugh, the second or third chart of the "new volunteers presentation" had this quotation from my dear great, great, great, great, great, (oh you get the idea) uncle, Dr. Benjamin Rush: "Let the doors be of iron, and let the grating, occasioned by opening and shutting them, be increased by an echo that shall deeply pierce the soul." Dr. Benjamin Rush, a signer of the Declaration of Independence, was quoted as saying this in 1787 regarding how a prison should be built. Little did he know that 200+ years later the echo of those iron doors would pierce my heart and soul.

You see, I was being trained to be a chaplain on the hospice wards of the prison. When I told the Office of Field Education at Duke Divinity School that I felt called to be a hospice chaplain, I wasn't thinking that one of my placements would be behind the prison walls! Yet that September, I found myself with more than fifty men who were dying or seriously ill behind the barbed wires of the prison. Mistakenly, I thought that I was bringing Christ to them. Instead, I quickly found out that they would *be Christ* for me.

These men at first overwhelmed my heart to such a degree that all I could do was sit – quite mute, mind you – and listen to them and cry. And cry I did as I heard their back stories. At times, we would just stare at each other with tears flowing down our eyes, knowing that words could not possibly explain or give any further clarity to the moment than our tears. No matter how difficult their back stories were, they told me how they found Christ and how they were hanging onto him with every fiber of their being.

Now, let me share something: These men were from every part of the country trying to get much-needed care for their cancer which was most likely at Stage 4. So, they most likely were thousands of miles away from family. They might have had very few personal possessions with them such as family pictures or even their own treasured Bible because those might have been caught in transit from one prison to this federal prison. They were also hundreds of miles away from cellmates who had become family to them. They were quite literally stripped of *everything* as they were dying. And so, when I say they were hanging onto Christ, I mean that they were *clinging* to Christ with their entire being. If you have ever seen a mother throw herself on top of her dying child and wail – well, that is the closest picture that I can give you.

One of the men that I became very close to was Hispanic. I can speak about three words of Spanish. He could only speak about three words of English. But none of that mattered. He literally would tell his nurse to hold his morphine until I had visited with him because he wanted to be fully awake for our visit. We would always end our time with me praying in English and then him praying in Spanish. I have no idea what he prayed, but the power of his prayers I could feel from the top of my head to the bottoms of my feet. Tears were always plentiful. The Holy Spirit always moved in a powerful way. When he died, I literally was inconsolable.

These men overwhelmed my heart. These men *transformed* my heart. They were, and still are, Christ to me. Every week as I went to the prison, I went looking for Christ in every single man that I met because I believe that every single person is born with the *Imago Dei* or the image of God within them. If there is a spark of God within each person, each man, then I am going to find it with God's help. I will love them, and I will pray for them until I see it. Without fail, I eventually saw it in each man that I met.

I will be going soon to Virginia's death row. This opportunity dropped out of nowhere for me. I received a random call from a lawyer in Virginia one day who had been told that I was the person to talk to in North Carolina about people who care about prison ministry. I once again am saying to God, "**Really**?!" I mean, it is a two-and-a-half-hour drive **one way** up there. As those of us who do prison ministry know, once you get there they can conjure a million reasons why you can't get in on that particular day. So, you might make the drive, only to be turned around. I am currently unemployed, so I do not have the financial means to make these trips happen; I therefore will need random people to donate dimes and quarters to help me. But, I am compelled to go. Compelled. Because I know that Christ is waiting – waiting so patiently for me to show up.

Isn't this what the season of Advent is all about? Crossing deserts to find the baby Jesus? Following the stars at night – through the intense darkness – to find the babe in the manger? Being transformed and overwhelmed by all that we see, feel, and touch? Having something new being born within us? Shouldn't we all be compelled to go and find Christ wherever Christ is? Will you go? Christ is waiting – waiting so patiently for us to show up.

Matthew 11:2-5

This again is one of my more personal stories. Jesus is making preposterous claims, or so it seems, as to whether he is actually the Messiah or not. In this piece, I share a poignant moment between a dear girlfriend who is dying and myself. You will see how I discovered we serve a God who is "upside down." Because of this, we should expect as we delve deeper into Scripture that our lives as well will be turned upside down.

> Matthew 11:2-5: "When John heard in prison what the Messiah was doing, he sent word by his disciples and said to him, "Are you the one who is to come, or are we to wait for another?" Jesus answered them, "Go and tell John what you hear and see: the blind receive their sight, the lame walk, the lepers are cleansed, the deaf hear, the dead are raised, and the poor have good news brought to them."

We find John the Baptist in prison. The man has been the heralder of the Good News that the Messiah has been born. He now is incarcerated and most likely chained to a wall behind an iron gate. Surely, he knew that King Herod was a jealous king and would not stand for another man to get the glory and honor. Therefore, John most likely knew that his days were numbered and his death would soon be coming as he sat shackled in his dank and dark prison cell.

As he nears death, he asks the question that so many ask at the end of their lives: "Are you the one who is to come, or are we to wait for another?" "Tell me once and for all Jesus, so that I am 100% sure. Are you the real deal or have I just been wasting my time proclaiming something that was not the truth? My time is almost up. I must know. I have to know."

And, Jesus replies: ""Go and tell John what you hear and see: the blind receive their sight, the lame walk, the lepers are cleansed, the deaf hear, the dead are raised, and the poor have good news brought to them." In other words, "Yes, John, I have turned the world upside down just like the prophet Isaiah said I would. I am the one. I **am** the one."

As my friend, Amy, was dying years ago, I crawled into the bed next to her. Amy no longer wanted people sitting next to her as it made it feel like she had to carry on a conversation which she absolutely had no energy for. So, I took off my shoes and snuggled up beside her. I put my head against hers and told her, "I think I will just nap with you if that's okay." With the faintest whisper, you could hear her relief, "Yes!"

Several minutes went by of just peaceful being together. Finally, Amy whispered to me, "What will it be like?" Speaking very softly to her, I said: "Ohhhhh. I love the picture that Henri Nouwen paints of it. He says you will be like a trapeze artist. You will be flying through the air going back and forth, back and forth, back and forth – you know with your beautiful black hair back on your head. And at some point, you will decide to let go. Not in a scary way, but in a peace-filled way. And just as you do, God will be there to scoop you up and to carry you back and forth, back and forth, and back and forth – you know God loves to have fun, too. And then at some point, you will land on the other side. You will be filled with joy, peace, and love. All will be well. All will be well."

"I like that," she whispered to me with a tear in her eye.

"I like that too," I whispered as I let the tears roll down my cheeks.

But here is the thing: As I was telling her the story and imagining it in my mind's eye with every ounce of my being so that she could see the same images I was seeing, I realized something: God had to be upside down in order to catch my dear friend. God had to be upside down!

Henri Nouwen will say it this way: "A flyer must fly, and a catcher must catch, and the flyer must trust, with outstretched arms, that his catcher will be there for him. The words of Jesus flashed through my mind, 'Father into your hands I commend my Spirit.'"[4]

Into God's hands, we can commend our spirits because we serve a God who turns our world upside down – where death doesn't have the final word, life does, where blindness to the truth doesn't have the final word, but illumination and revelation do, where groveling to get to God doesn't have the final word, but walking in the belovedness of love does, where sin and leper spots don't have the final word, but holiness and righteousness do, and where scarcity and lack do not have the final word, but an overabundance beyond our wildest imagination does.

May we walk in the truth that our God will go to whatever length needed – even hanging upside down on a trapeze bar – in order to catch us, to keep us, to love us, and to welcome us into God's beloved community and to say to us those most precious words, "you are my beloved in whom I am well pleased."

---

[4] Nouwen, Henri J. M., *Our Greatest Gift: A meditation on Dying and Caring*, New York, New York, HarperCollins Publisher, 1985, 67.

1 Samuel 3:10

In this story, I speak deeply from my own narrative and how I have learned a lot about what it means to truly listen to God and to listen to the God in each other.

> 1 Samuel 3:10: "Speak, for your servant is listening."

For a year and a half, I learned how to listen and listen intently at a Veterans Administration hospital. I learned to listen quite literally in the dark with veterans as they told their tales of unbelievable trauma. I listened to women week after week as they talked about the horrors of military sexual trauma. I listened to families who mourned and grieved greatly at the sudden death of one they loved so very deeply. I listened to veterans who had attempted suicide multiple times and who wanted to try it one more time because what was going on inside their head just would not stop. I listened. I showed up and I listened. By the end of my time there, I called myself the "6-foot ear."

And then for two years, I participated in a Spiritual Direction program where I learned how to listen again. This time, I was told to listen *with* the Holy Spirit; save an extra chair for the Spirit to show up, sit down, and speak from. I learned seemingly hundreds of spiritual practices on how to listen both to the Spirit that dwells within as well as to the speaker who is speaking. I listened. I was intentional about my listening.

However, God has reminded me more than once that listening to God means one deliberate act after another deliberate act. It is a turning off of distractions and a turning on of your ears. It is a turning off of the noise between your ears and a turning on of Christ's peace. It is a turning off of your own agenda and a turning on of God's presence. It is a turning off of the many things that clamor for attention when you least expect it and a turning on of stillness. It is a turning off of doubts of self-worth and a turning on of "I am your beloved in whom you are well pleased." It is a turning off of all devices that buzz and ring and a turning on of the Spirit who loves to dance and sing. It is a turning off of anything *not* God and turning one's whole being *to* God.

Then, we can finally say "Speak, for your servant is listening." God, I give you my full attention. There is nothing else that matters other than hearing from you. It is your voice and your voice alone that I seek. It is that small, quiet whisper that grounds me and shows me which way to go in life. I simply cannot do it on my own as you are the very air that I breathe in and breathe out. Please, God, speak. Speak softly. Speak tenderly. Speak clearly. For your servant is listening.

Deuteronomy 8:2

Here again, I use my current situation to allow God to speak and to speak clearly to me. Whenever Scripture goes "Krrrplop," it usually means that God is actively trying to get your attention. It is easy just to wander away and not see what God is trying to tell you. The harder path for many of us is to allow Scripture to land in your lap, to stare it in the face, to welcome it into your arms, and to open your heart to what it wants to share with you – good or bad, happy or sad, welcome or unwelcome.

"Krrrrrr-plop!!!!!"

This morning as I was reading my morning Scripture and prayers, I was given Deuteronomy 8:2-16 to read (By the way, I haven't figured out which translation they use but, in case you were wondering, it is the "Daily Prayer" app that I use).

The first few words were "Remember the long way…"

I simply lost my breath.

"Remember the long way that the Lord your God has led you…"

Yes, these ten years have indeed been the *long way* because of my mystery illness. And before you hear a theology that says, "God caused me to be sick," please stop. God is not in the "make sick" or "make die" business. God is in the "re" business – redeeming, reclaiming, remaking, redoing, rebuilding, reviving, and yes, resurrecting business. God is a God of life. God is a God of love.

But God can also be a God of loooonnnnnggg ways. God is the *Alpha* and *Omega* – the beginning and the end. All at the same time, God somehow holds the beginning and the end together because our God is a God outside of our time; our loooonnnnnggg ways are but twinkles in God's eyes. And so what is ten years to God?

I have often thought about Matthew 13:23:

> "But the seed falling on good soil refers to someone who hears the word and understands it. This is the one who produces a crop, yielding a hundred, sixty, or thirty times what was sown."

Some preachers preach this as some sort of prosperity gospel. But what if Jesus is actually talking about these being deeper steps into the life of Christ? What if this is the *long way* into the heart of God?

You see, I learned a lot about God and God's heart when I walked 30 steps in. I felt like I was truly who God meant for me to be. But when I walked 60 steps into the heart and mind of Christ, I realized I was just scratching the surface back when I just walked the 30 steps. But, as I landed at the 60, I stopped, praised God for all I had learned and felt like I had arrived. Now that I am 100 steps into my journey, I realize the journey into the heart of God is a very long way; it is, in fact, a lifelong journey. Along the way, God is redeeming, reclaiming, remaking, redoing, rebuilding, reviving, and yes, resurrecting, all that is broken within me, bit by bit, piece by piece.

I don't know if you have ever walked a labyrinth, but I will never forget walking the "really long part" to then, all of the sudden, have to make a "U-turn." I stopped and literally said aloud, "God, I don't want to go back - I don't want to feel like I am backtracking - I want to go straight away - don't make me turn around." There I stood. (Thankfully, I was alone!) Something within me said, "accept it with grace." As tears flowed down my cheeks, I made my U-turn and kept walking. Of course, I eventually found my way to the center — with all the U-turns made. And then I walked into the center of what I thought of as God's heart where a massive rock sat with other little rocks atop it. There were small pieces of paper wedged in-between the cracks, all of which I imagined signified prayer requests or heavy burdens that others were leaving there - leaving there on God's heart. I sat on the rock and wept some more. And yes, I didn't want to venture back out of the maze the same way I came in, but eventually I found the grace to do that, too.

As people of God, we are called to longer paths to destinations unknown. But God's call never changes; God's call is simply "Follow me." "Follow me." Hmmm; truly, that is all I need to know.

Matthew 11:28-30: Write your own sermon for those on the inside

This sermon shows you how you can take just a few sentences out of Scripture and chew on them for weeks on end in order to have God enlighten you on the countless nuances of the Scripture. For instance, we read the word "rest" twice and the word "burden" twice. We might think in our English translation that we are only dealing with two words. However, upon deeper study, I learned that, in the Greek, there are actually four words and not just two. So, there are two different words for "rest" and two different words for "burden." This knowledge made the Scripture come alive to me. As you will see, my own life experience at the time of literally being "one handed" also made this Scripture very real to me.

Matthew 11:28-30

> "Come to me, all you who are weary and burdened, and I will give you rest. Take my yoke upon you and learn from me, for I am gentle and humble in heart, and you will find rest for your souls. For my yoke is easy and my burden is light."

Prayer: Gracious God and Creator of Sabbath rest, may we enter into your peace, may we enter into your rest even now. May these words fall like snowflakes, gently and softly upon our lives. May your word touch each heart as uniquely as each of those snowflakes are made – as uniquely as each one of us is made in your image. Thank you for your sweet and abiding presence with us. In Christ's name, we pray. Amen.

On Ash Wednesday, I fell and broke my collarbone. Instead of a yoke, I received a sling to wear around my right arm so that I could not, and would not, use it. I do everything with my right arm. I brush my teeth with my right arm. I open lids that seal things shut with my right arm. I turn faucets on and off with my right arm. I sign my name to checks with my right arm. I type these words I am writing with my right arm. I dust and sweep with my right arm. I turn the pages of my books with my right arm. I hold my coffee with my right arm. I pick up my jug of sweet tea with my right arm. I dry my hair with my right arm. I pick up the hangers filled with clothes with my right arm. I do everything... with my right arm. My world is a right-armed world and I know nothing else. Wellllllll, I knew nothing else...

After that fateful fall, I was faced with not only being left-handed, but being one-handed. This world was completely new and bizarre to me. I mean, how does one realllllly brush their teeth with their left hand? For instance, after what I thought was a complete and thorough scrubbing of my teeth, I did one of those "tongue checks." You know what I mean, right? You run your tongue along your teeth to make sure that you didn't miss any little section. And I should not have been surprised that day after day, I was failing miserably. Therefore, I had to discipline myself to be even more intentional with my brushing of my teeth. I had to stop, concentrate, and live into every single tooth as if it had a life of its own. Ahhhh, then I could pass the "tongue check."

I was learning to live this intentionally for practically every – single – little – itsy – bitsy – thing – that I did. This great intentionality ended up being a great Lenten practice for me. The one thing I learned the **most** is that I cannot do it alone. John Donne reminds us, "No man is an island." Each of us belongs to one another. I belong to you and you belong to me. We need each other. We intentionally need each other.

Therefore, it should not be shocking to us that yokes have *two* slots for heads to go through – one for me and one for you. Or, if we want to share our burdens with God – well, there is one slot for God and one slot for us. In this way, our burdens are lighter. Those who are weary are less so. In the midst of the chaos of life, we thankfully can and will find rest.

And yet, how often have I been walking around with this yoke hanging around my neck, you know with the other side open and dangling off to one side? There I am for everyone to see – you know, just dragging this two-slotted yoke around by myself because I want to prove to the world how strong I am, how I can fend for myself, how self-sufficient I am, and how I have no need for anyone else. Of course, Scripture whaps me in the face with the words of Paul in 1 Corinthians 12:21: "The eye cannot say to the hand, 'I don't need you!' And the head cannot say to the feet, 'I don't need you!'" Ah, we need someone to fill that open slot in our yoke. If we take a long hard look in the mirror at ourselves, we realize how absolutely ridiculous we look walking around with a two-slotted yoke and just one head filling it.

I always try to "live into the narrative" – walk around in it – put myself in the scene – play each character. I realized as I was living into this scene that, as we carry each other's burdens, we can't look each other in the face. Rather, we have to be "all ears" to hear what the other person is going through. We have to be attentive and intentional about listening. Since we are talking straight ahead versus face to face, each of us might have to either speak up a bit or, orrrrrrr, we might have to lean in and listen with your entire being so that we don't miss a single syllable. This kind of listening is very difficult for most people and so it is a learned act – a learned behavior – and only learned by a "repeat performance." We must be willing to intentionally listen over and over and over again.

As a Chaplain intern inside the prison on the hospice wards, I was asked to write up "verbatims" of my conversations with the guys I had talked to. My supervisor at the time was going through Chaplaincy training and was learning all about verbatims and how to be "all ears," so he thought it would be an awesome practice for me, too. I found out very quickly that it is indeed a wonderful practice but a humbling practice as well. You see, when you have to write down "verbatim" what you told someone and what they told you, all of the sudden you are much more aware of every single little word you say and every small behavior you do. That year, I learned how to be a much better listener and how to lean in and be "all ears."

I also had to confront those times where I tuned out the speaker and went into my own world. I had to ask myself repeatedly why that was and what made me leave *their* conversation with them to concentrate on what was going on inside *my* head. It was very overwhelming and soul-wrenching at times, I must say. But I learned a lot about my own "inner darkness," my "shadow" side that I wanted to deny even existed. Yet, with those silly and humbling verbatims, my shadow just stared at me like a dog waiting to go outside for a walk or wanting to eat – you know that long stare with no blinking - no hesitation – just full-on stare. Therefore, I had to confront a lot of things lurking in the dark recesses of my mind and soul which turned out to be pure grace for me. However, it was tough going through it.

Another thing that hit me when I was living into the scene of this Scripture picturing me and a friend, or me and God, being yoked together: I realized that all we can do for each other is walk with each other side by side – just walk – just journey – just be there for each step – just be there for each turn – you know, in lock step with one another – following the same rhythm, the same pace.

I have shared with many of my friends what is most helpful while I am waiting for my broken collarbone to heal is actually just their mere presence. This scares a lot of people. We are a society of "doers," of "fixers," of "rescuers," and of "helpers."

"What do you mean you want me to just be present?" my friend would say. "I don't have to bring anything over?"
"Nope, no need."
"But, don't you want me to take you somewhere."
"Nope, I am good."
"Then, what do you want me to do?"
"Just be with me."

154

Just "being" with someone who is seriously ill makes some people very anxious. Some people feel that they can only be with me when I am feeling better, but that isn't what Jesus meant. We really need to share the yoke when we have a burden to share, when life gets tough, when we are going through it. When we feel like we cannot take the next step alone. When we wonder if anyone else cares.

In his amazingly vulnerable book, *Lament for a Son*, Nicholas Wolterstorff puts it this way:

> "Put your hand into my wounds," said the risen Jesus to Thomas, "and you will know who I am." ... So, I shall struggle to live the reality of Christ's rising and death's dying. In my living, my son's dying will not be the last word. But as I rise up, I bear the wounds of his death. My rising does not remove them. They mark me. If you want to know who I am, put your hands in.[5]

If you want to know who I am, put your hands in. Or, as Jesus is saying in Matthew 11:28-30, put your *head* in. Put your head in the yoke and help me shoulder the load. Put your head in and be open to where the other person takes you. Put your head in and be open to another person's suffering.

I realized that there is a mutuality here when you put your head in. Not only are you sharing in another person's suffering and burdens, but they are helping to carry yours, too. You lighten the loads for each other just by the simple act of putting your heads in the yoke. This calls for an authenticity of one's personhood – a vulnerability to share what is going on in one's life. Many friends, as they came over and just sat with me a spell or two would tell me as they were leaving, "Wow, I feel so much better and here I came to help you feel better." That is the mutuality of sharing burdens – of sharing the yoke. In the midst of it, the miraculous happens, and you are

---

[5] Wolterstorff, Nicholas, *Lament for a Son*, Grand Rapids, MI, William B. Eerdmans Publishing Company, 1987, 92-93.

both healed because you both have shared together the yoke. You both have found needed rest for your souls.

Another thing that hit me as I was living into the scene and thinking of my own sling – a lot of people want to yank the yoke off. I mean it would be easier, right, if you did not have that big old yoke around your neck to begin with! "So, here, let me help you – I will yank it off and everything will be better." I had a very "helpful" person try and take my sling off for me. They saw me struggle a little bit, so they ran to the rescue, because they love me so very, very much, and they yanked off my sling. However, in doing so, they made my injury worse – my pain went skyrocketing – and absolutely nothing was better. What I needed was a patient presence to just be there with me.

The truth is for all of us, when we see someone else with this big yoke around their neck we want their suffering to end – we want their pain to stop – we want to fix the situation somehow and in some way. Suffering makes us nervous, it plays havoc on our anxieties, and so we end up yanking the yoke off instead of seeing that there is another hole – a hole left for our head to go through – a hole left there for us to help carry the burden – a hole left there for making the burden much lighter. And so we fix the issue for them and in doing so, all we do is make their problems even worse. The harder thing for us to do is to stop, breathe deeply, and then ask the person, "is there something I could do to help or do you have it?"

I will confess that I used to shoulder a lot of worries and cares on my own, so it is no wonder that my collarbone broke at the weight of it. It was an awful thing, actually. For all of my years learning hundreds of various spiritual practices, I just kept shouldering the cares and worries of so many. Therefore, with the urging of many of my close friends, the new practice I have started is telling other people my needs. I just throw them out there with wild abandon. Some things get picked up. Others do not. But even the act of telling people what I need keeps me grounded in the reality that there is another hole in the yoke. And if I wait patiently enough, someone will come by and fill up the space. Almost always someone will help me to "shoulder on."

I also realized that this passage states that we are to rest twice. Rest. Rest. But how many of us actually rest? Or, if we do rest, how guilty do we feel that we wore our jammies all day long? I found it interesting that there are two different Greek words here for rest – one means to "remain" and the other means to "cease from doing."

The first sentence "Come to me... I will give you rest" is the one which means "remain." And this should not be surprising really that as we come to Jesus that we are to abide there – we are to remain there – we are to take root there. Jesus is always calling us to "follow me" – "abide with me" – "remain with me" – "come to me" – and when you do I – will – give - you - rest.

And the second rest means to "cease from doing" *after* you put on the yoke. Now, picture this with me because I am imagining that you have two cows and you put the yoke on them in order to till the ground. And instead of them plodding through the dirt as good and obedient cows should do, they both take the grand opportunity to take a nap as soon as the yoke goes on! This is what Jesus is saying to us, "with my yoke, you will be able to cease from doing – you will be able to finally rest." For Jesus will say his yoke is easy in that he will supply all of our needs and his burdens are light.

Notice also with me that Jesus uses the word "burdens" twice. The first burden means "to load up, to load on spiritual anxiety, to be overburdened with ceremony, to lay on heavy the Mosaic Law and the tradition that goes with it." So, all of that in which you read in the Old Testament – Jesus is saying once again "forget about it. You all have heaped too much extra stuff on. It is overburdening you. Do not follow it anymore."

The second word for "burden" means to follow Jesus' commandments. And Jesus was really clear that there were just a few commandments: Love God. Love one another. Love your enemy. Simple dimple, right? Jesus is saying in essence "Go Love! Go Love!" But let's be real, even these burdens are not light! Even loving God isn't simple at times. Loving others can be a challenge especially those who are vastly different from you – culturally different – or hmmmm, maybe even when they are exactttttly like you!

And then the whole loving one's enemies always trips us up, especially the more personal the enemy is – the closer the harm, the more difficult the love. And yet Jesus says, "love your enemies – loving friends and family, wellllll, that is easy, you need to cross over to the other side of the road and show love to your enemies too."

Let me be really clear about something though; this is something that will never, ever be done without being yoked to Christ. Let me repeat that: Loving one's enemies, especially if the harm is close up and personal, will never, ever happen unless you are yoked with Christ. You need to be abiding with Christ. You need to be relying on Christ. You need Christ to *shoulder* that burden with you. You cannot do it alone.

Let me rephrase this Scripture for you with the Greek fully defined for "rest" and "burden": "Come to me, all you who are weary and burdened with the old Mosaic law that gives you spiritual anxiety, and I will give you an abiding rest. Take my yoke upon you and learn from me, for I am gentle and humble in heart, and you will find rest where you cease from doing anything for your souls. For my yoke is easy and my burden of loving God and loving one another is light."

One last thought as I lived into this scene and as I was dragging around this yoke with one side dangling off of my neck: Jesus asked me, "When are you going to ask me to stand beside you? To stand with you? To remain with you? To abide with you? When are you

158

going to ask for my presence?" And Jesus continued in no uncertain terms, "You and I must be yoked."

Did you hear what I am saying? As Bishop Ken Carder, my dear friend, will say, "God wants us to be yoked with God's amazing and astounding love!" Isn't this the Gospel message!? God wants us to yoke with God's amazing love – that unconditional, cup-overflowing, unbounded mercy, nonjudgmental, flowing freely through us and out of us to others, carrying the burden of love! That way, we can be with those who are forgotten and stand against the powers that would oppress them.

This is a love that says even to our enemies:
- Let me show you love by giftwrapping my favorite outfit so you can wear it to church next Sunday.
- Let me love others like a river that flows through us and breaks down barriers at the sheer strength of its force.
- Let me search for a love that resurrects alllllll that is dead, *whatever* it is, and brings it to life – **to life**.
- Let my eyes of love sees others for all eternity through the eyes of grace – just of grace.
- Let me use the words of love that say to all of us as we emerge from those baptismal waters, "You are **my Beloved** in whom I am well pleased."

We are to be yoked with **this** love – with Jesus' love – all day, every day.

While it was an accident that on the first day of Lent that I broke my collar bone, it was not an accident that God has redeemed my time on my couch to teach me a few things.

I needed to learn a deeper intentionality to my life.

I needed to see that in someone carrying my load, I was carrying *their* load, too. As they were present for me, I was also present for them. As they were all ears for me, I was all ears for them.

159

I needed to learn that all of this shouldering-by-myself business was getting me absolutely nowhere. I needed to learn to share my burdens with others who were more than able (and quite happily so) to share my load with me.

I needed to be reminded that we are to abide, in a very rooted sense, with Jesus all throughout our day. This kind of abiding would give me the real rest I needed where I didn't have to do anything but be with Jesus.

I needed to relearn to follow Jesus' commandments to love – to really love – to be yoked to love - and to rest that Jesus could and would love through me. As I let Jesus' love flow through me, I could in turn be the source of love for those I am with.

And then, and then, in this way, I can - we can, be Christ for one another exactly at the moment when we truly need Christ to show up.

May it be so. May it be so. Amen and Amen.

Write your own sacred texts story

PART 3. APPENDIXES

Appendix A. Teaching this book as a class

I have used the contents of this book for class materials several times. I recommend that you follow the sequence that the chapters indicate: Luke 15, Psalm 23, and so on. I find that there is something sacred about people talking first about their own "lostness" as well as being found by God. The theme of shepherd then lends itself well for looking at Psalm 23. Psalm 23's thread of walking through the dark valleys makes an amazing segue to looking at Mary "pre-dawn" and being asked "Woman, why are you weeping?" in John 20. Following that with the 1 Samuel 16 story, about how God calls those not even in the room, is a powerful next step. By this time, people should be used to writing their own story and so can then use anything as a sacred text – a poem, something from the Quran, a saying from a theologian or saint, and/or a saying from a mystic.

Allow at least one hour for each class. For the first class, please allow at least an hour and a half due to the amount of information that you are giving and getting from the participants.

A class syllabus would look something like this:

Class 1

- Start with prayer. You can either say your own or read a prayer that you find particularly meaningful. If you read the prayer, I suggest having copies of the prayer for all class members.
- Hand out "Appendix E. Group guidelines" (page 177) to all of the group participants and gain their agreement to the guidelines. Feel free to add any items as the group thinks necessary.

- Use a writing exercise where people write out a short introduction of themselves. They will then read their introduction to the class. This helps people start the sharing of their own life stories to others in a concise yet meaningful way.
- Read the "Overview" (page 2) out loud to the class. After reading it, make sure that the process is understood by the class participants. Remind them too that you will be using the process over and over again, so it will become obvious over time if at first they don't understand it fully.
- Read the Lost Sheep-Lost Coin (page 11) out loud – twice and very slowly.
- Read the questions about the Lost Sheep-Lost Coin. Hint: Don't read all of them. Read enough of them so that each class member resonates with at least one question. This will require you to read the questions first and highlight the questions that *you* think are the most meaningful. Remember to keep your audience in mind as you do this. What resonates with someone who might be homeless will likely differ from what resonates for someone who lives in a beautiful home.
- Discuss the assignment for writing your story. This is the only time that I read one of my writings first. I do this so people can "hear" what the assignment is all about. Telling your class members what kind of story you are hoping that you want them to write is not as effective as them being able to hear for themselves what you are after. Also, let them know, that whatever they write it will be perfect. Long or short, vulnerable or factual, well written or barely cobbled together – whatever they come up with, it is perfect.

Class 2
- Start with prayer.

- Share the "Lost" writings with one other. You can use the spiritual direction process for this found in Appendix C (page 170).
- Say a prayer that incorporates a part of each story as a gift to the broader group.
- Read Psalm 23 twice very slowly.
- Read Psalm 23 questions.
- Discuss the assignment for each participant writing his or her own story.
- Check in on how the writing and reflecting is going.

Class 3

- Start with prayer.
- Share Psalm 23 stories with each other, again using the spiritual direction process.
- Say a prayer that incorporates a part of each story as a gift to the broader group.
- Read John 20, "Woman, why are you weeping?" twice very slowly.
- Read John 20 questions.
- Discuss the assignment for each participant writing his or her own story.

Class 4

- Start with prayer.
- Share John 20 stories with each other.
- Say a prayer that incorporates each story as a gift to the broader group.
- Read 1 Samuel 16 twice very slowly.
- Read 1 Samuel 16 questions.
- Discuss the assignment for each participant writing his or her own story.

Class 5

- Start with prayer.
- Share 1 Samuel 16 stories with each other.
- Say a prayer that incorporates a part of each story as a gift to the broader group.
- Share sacred texts very slowly. Hint: you can use the Scripture provided in my book or you can make up your own.
- Share how you can take one or two lines of Scripture (or any text you find *sacred*) and see how it can make you feel like you just can't breathe **or** that it refreshes your soul or a myriad of feelings!
- Discuss the assignment for each participant writing his or her own story based upon whatever sacred text the class member wants.

Class 6

- Start with a prayer.
- Share sacred text stories.
- Say a prayer that incorporates a part of each story as a gift to the broader group.
- Teach how to run the class as a circle, a spiritual direction group, a class, or a combination of the group formats.
- End with prayer.

Use the same hints for the spiritual direction process for the class (Appendix C, page 170). A handout for these helpful hints can be found in "Appendix E. Group guidelines" (page 177). If people do not want to read their writing, this is perfectly fine. The class brings forward a lot of feelings, especially unwanted ones, for the class members. Each person needs to feel that the space is sacred space where they can lend their voice or simply listen to the reflections and stories of others.

I also suggest that you have facial tissues for these groups; they can be quite emotional for all in attendance.

After the class ends, you can suggest starting a spiritual direction group so that they can continue their time together. The details of what a group would look like are in Appendix C, page 170. I have found that most people want to stay together, if at all possible, because they have already established great trust with those in the class.

Appendix B. Helpful hints for your class-sharing time

These are hints for the teacher to use when teaching this as a class or as a spiritual direction group (explained in "Appendix C. Using this book in a spiritual direction group," page 170):

1. The leader for the class (or for the day) should come well prepared. Be prepared with class materials as well as with your heart open ready to receive.
2. Gain agreement from each participant that the group will be a *confidential* group. There is to be no sharing of anything shared in the group outside the group.
3. If someone wants to ask a question about what another participant said, they should go to them when the group is not in session.
   The group's main purpose is for intently listening to one another's stories and not to question each other, judge, or disagree with what someone is doing or saying. If needed, the student can jot quick questions down on a piece of paper for future reference. Remember, this process is used to help the class members be much more intentional about listening deeply to their peers, listening deeply to God, and to also be heard by others.
4. Allow each person to be deeply heard through the telling of their story. Ensure that there is both time for each person to share as well as for silence between the stories.
5. Ask someone to be your timekeeper. Do a bit of quick math and divide up the time before you begin and stick to those minutes. Over time, people become better able to regulate themselves and a timekeeper will be unnecessary.
6. Agree to start on time. If you do not start on time, then someone's time gets squeezed and it is not fair to them.

Decide how you will handle late-comers: Will they be able to attend? Will they be able to slip in quietly?

7.   Remind the participants that the reason for silence between the speaking is a way to honor and to integrate what the person has just said. You usually have one person who just can't wait to speak, so reminding the group of the overall goals and guidelines for the first few gatherings is important.

8.   Let everyone know that if for whatever reason they do not feel comfortable sharing one week that it is absolutely fine. No one is judged for staying silent. Everyone will be silent at least one week, most likely.

9.   Around the third or fourth meeting, after everyone has shared ask the group, ask your group members if they feel anything needs to change with the group. This gives people a chance to alter what is going on and to feel ownership of their group.

10. Keep your group small (6-8 people) so trust and confidentiality are easily maintained. This also gives each person plenty of time to share their story within the hour.

NOTE: You can make copies and distribute "Appendix E. Group guidelines" (page 177) to your group members as a handout.

Appendix C. Using this book in a spiritual direction group

If you want to start a spiritual direction group (some people call this a "circle"), the "Living into the Narrative of God" process lends itself very well to that. An ideal spiritual direction group is comprised of no more than eight people. You want the group to be small enough so that trust, safety, and confidence can be built quickly amongst all members of the group. The ideal amount of time for the group is one hour.

The process would go something like this:

Open with everyone sitting in a circle.

Then have at least a minute to preferably 3 minutes of silence.

The leader says an opening prayer. The prayer should include welcoming the Holy Spirit into the space and asking the Holy Spirit to speak clearly to the group and through those gathered.

Hand out "Appendix E. Group guidelines" (page 177) to all of the group participants and gain their agreement to the guidelines. Feel free to add any items as the group thinks necessary.

The leader of the day (this is a rotated assignment) reads Scripture. (The Scripture text should not be long, but it could be an entire Psalm like Psalm 23).

Psalm 23

[1] The Lord is my shepherd, I lack nothing.
[2]   He makes me lie down in green pastures,
he leads me beside quiet waters,
[3]   he refreshes my soul.
He guides me along the right paths
    for his name's sake.

⁴ Even though I walk
  through the darkest valley,
I will fear no evil,
  for you are with me;
your rod and your staff,
  they comfort me.
⁵ You prepare a table before me
  in the presence of my enemies.
You anoint my head with oil;
  my cup overflows.
⁶ Surely your goodness and love will follow me
  all the days of my life,
and I will dwell in the house of the Lord
  forever.

Then, the leader states how the Scripture has affected him or her personally through a personal story. For this, select a story that you have written or one that you have in your heart from the Scripture to share. (The sharing by the leader should take no longer than 5 minutes.)

Moment of silence: Usually, try to take 1 minute between speakers in order to honor the words of the speaker, to reflect deeply on what was said, and to hold up to God what requests you might feel are on their heart.

Another person speaks about how the Scripture spoke to them. Each person should take about 5 minutes depending upon how many people are in your group.

Moment of silence: Again, try to take 1 minute.

Continue until all who want to speak do so.

Moment of silence.

The leader ends with a prayer trying to incorporate the things that each person has said and bringing all of the requests and all of the stories to God.

End.

NOTE: Use the suggestions in "Appendix B. Helpful hints for your class-sharing time" (page 168). A handout for these guidelines can be found on the last page of this book.

This process will only take a few sessions before everyone gets the rhythm for their time together. For the first couple of spiritual direction groups, start with the helpful hints in Appendix B in order to level-set the group on how to make the most out of each group session.

Appendix D. Using this book for a retreat

You can use this book for a three-day retreat. I suggest that you start on a Friday evening and end on Sunday. The class syllabus would look like this:

Class 1 (Friday night)

- Start with prayer. You can either say your own or read a prayer that you find particularly meaningful. If you read the prayer, I suggest having copies of the prayer for all class members.
- Hand out "Appendix E. Group guidelines" (page 177) to all of the group participants and gain their agreement to the guidelines. Feel free to add any items as the group thinks necessary.
- Use a writing exercise where people write out a short introduction of themselves. They will then read their introduction to the class. This helps people start the sharing of their own life stories to others in a concise yet meaningful way.
- Read the "Overview" (page 2) out loud to the class. After reading it, make sure that the process is understood by the class participants. Remind them too that you will be using the process over and over again, so it will become obvious over time if at first they don't understand it fully.
- Read the Lost Sheep-Lost Coin (page 11) out loud – twice and very slowly.
- Read the questions about the Lost Sheep-Lost Coin. Hint: Don't read all of them. Read enough of them so that each class member resonates with at least one question. This will require you to read the questions first and highlight the questions that *you* think are the most meaningful.

Remember to keep your audience in mind as you do this. What resonates with someone who might be homeless will likely differ from what resonates for someone who lives in a beautiful home.

- Discuss the assignment for writing your story. This is the only time that I read one of my writings first. I do this so people can "hear" what the assignment is all about. Telling your class members what kind of story you are hoping that you want them to write is not as effective as them being able to hear for themselves what you are after. Also, let them know, that whatever they write it will be perfect. Long or short, vulnerable or factual, well written or barely cobbled together – whatever they come up with, it is perfect.

Class 2 (8:00 AM, Saturday morning)

- Start with prayer.
- Share "Lost" writing with each other. You can use the spiritual direction group process for this.
- The leader says a prayer that incorporates part of each story as a gift to the broader group.
- Read Psalm 23 twice very slowly.
- Read Psalm 23 questions.
- Discuss the assignment for writing your own story.
- Check in on how the writing-reflecting is going.

Break for reflection, writing time, and lunch.

Class 3 (1:00 PM, Saturday afternoon)

- Start with prayer.
- Share Psalm 23 stories with each other (again, using the spiritual direction group process).

- Say a prayer that incorporates part of each story as a gift to the broader group.
- Read John 20 "Woman, why are you weeping?" twice very slowly.
- Read John 20 questions.
- Discuss the assignment for writing your own story.

Break for reflection, writing time, and dinner.

Class 4 (7:00 PM, Saturday night)
- Start with prayer.
- Share John 20 stories with each other.
- Say a prayer that incorporates part of each story as a gift to the broader group.
- Read 1 Samuel 16 twice very slowly.
- Read 1 Samuel 16 questions.
- Discuss the assignment for writing your own story.

Break for the evening and, hopefully get a good night's rest.

Prior to Class 5 on Sunday morning, gather for breakfast. Allow time for writing and reflection.

Class 5 (10:00 AM, Sunday morning)
- Start with prayer.
- Share 1 Samuel 16 stories with each other.
- Say a prayer that incorporates some part of each story as a gift to the broader group.
- Share sacred texts very slowly. You can use my list or make up your own.
- Share how you can take one or two lines of Scripture (or any text you find *sacred*) and see how sacred text can make

you feel like you just can't breathe **or** that it refreshes your soul or a myriad of feelings!

- Discuss the assignment for writing your own story based upon whatever sacred text each class member wants.

Hint: You might want to use Class 5 for some type of worship service together.

Break for writing, reflection, and lunch.

Class 6 (1:00 PM, Sunday morning)

- Start with a prayer.
- Share sacred text stories.
- Say a prayer that incorporates part of each story as a gift to the broader group.
- Teach how to run the class as a circle, a spiritual direction group, and/or a class.
- End with prayer.

I suggest that you have tissues for these groups as the sessions can be quite emotional for all.

In the advertising for the retreat, make it clear that the retreat will be an intense writing and reflection workshop and that each participant will need to be ready to write a lot about their own personal narrative.

Appendix E. Group guidelines

1. I agree to not share anything said within the group with any other person other than the person who spoke. Keeping everything as confidential, I understand, is foundational to our group.

2. I agree to listen deeply to another person's story without interrupting them, lending a judgment, or asking questions. I understand that part of what I will learn in this group is how to improve my listening skills. I will listen with my heart as well as my head. I will hold each story as sacred.

3. If asked to be the leader of the group, I will come fully prepared both physically and spiritually. I understand, too, that as the leader I will be called upon to say a prayer after all stories are shared. The prayer will offer back to God some piece of everyone's story. Therefore, I will listen very intently and deeply to each person's story ensuring not one story is left out.

4. If I have a question to ask one of the group members about their story, I will hold the question until after the group and go directly to the person. I will not talk about another person's story to anyone other than the one who shared the story.

5. I will maintain at least 1 minute of silence between each story. I understand that this is a way to honor that story by replaying the scenes or words most impactful to me.

6. I will show up to our group either early or on time. I understand that this is the way I can show my love and respect for our group.

7. I understand that I am not expected to share my story every week. If I just want to deeply hear others' stories, I will simply make an "x" with my arms over my heart or some other sign to let others know I will not be speaking.

Made in the USA
Columbia, SC
31 May 2021